P9-BHS-766

This is the
POODLE

LESTER H. MARTIN

Distributed in the U.S.A. by T.F.H. Publications, Inc., 211 West Sylvania Avenue, P.O. Box 27, Neptune City, N.J. 07753; in England by T.F.H. (Gt. Britain) Ltd., 13 Nutley Lane, Reigate, Surrey; in Canada by Clarke, Irwin & Company, Clarwin House, 791 St. Clair Avenue West, Toronto 10, Ontario; in Southeast Asia by Y. W. Ong, 9 Lorong 36 Geylang, Singapore 14; in Australia and the south Pacific by Pet Imports Pty. Ltd., P.O. Box 149, Brookvale 2100, N.S.W., Australia.
Published by T.F.H. Publications, Inc. Ltd., The British Crown Colony of Hong Kong.

AUTHOR'S NOTE

After I had written several chapters of this book, I consulted my old friend and long time associate, Dr. Leon F. Whitney who is general editor of this series of books. There were so many phases of breeding and reproduction, feeding and veterinary care about which he knew so much more than I that I asked him to write several chapters and permit me to use that material in this book in the hope that it would make the most complete and useful Poodle book which has ever been published. Dr. Leon Whitney wrote to his cousin, Dr. David D. Whitney who in turn permitted us to use the results of his studies in the inheritance of coat colors which I feel adds a great deal to the value of this book. I am deeply indebted to both of these gentlemen as I am to my present associate, Dr. George D. Whitney who has also made valuable suggestions.

Naturally my thanks go to the photographers, professional and amateur who supplied the excellent illustrations and to Dr. Herbert Axelrod and his wife Evelyn who planned the book and saw it through to completion.

ACKNOWLEDGEMENTS

Evelyn Shafer photos, pages 6, 7, 8, 9, 10, 11, 12, 13, 14, 20, 21, 22, 23, 24, 25, 26, 27, 28, 30, 31, 32, 33, 34, 35, 36, 37, 38, 40, 41, 42, 46, 48, 62, 64, 65, 67, 69, 70, 71, 72, 73, 75, 76, 77, 78, 80, 81, 86, 88, 89, 90, 91, 92, 93, 94, 95, 99, 100, 101, 102, 103, 105, 106, 107, 108, 109, 110, 112, 113, 118, 119, 120, 121, 123, 124, 125, 126, 127, 128, 129, 130, 131, 132, 133, 134, 135, 136, 137, 138, 139, 140, 141, 142, 143, 144, 145, 146, 147, 148, 149, 151, 152, 157, 181, 182.

Louise Van der Meid, photos, pages 39, 47, 51, 56, 58, 87, 104, 114, 115, 116, 122, 150, 153, 155, 185.

Three Lions Inc., George Pickow photos, pages 74, 82, 83, 84, 85, 117, 156, 169, 170, 171, 172, 173, 177, 179, 187, 191, 192, 193, 194, 195, 198, 199, 200, 210, 215.

Frasie Studio photos, pages 49, 50.

Ernest H. Hart drawings.

ISBN 0-87666-361-7

Copyright © 1960, by T.F.H. Publications, Inc.
Printed in the United States of America. All rights reserved.
This book, or parts thereof, may not be reproduced in any
form without permission of the publisher.

Contents

POODLE

1. Feet 2. Forelegs 3. Chest 4. Ear Feather
5. Lips 6. Muzzle 7. Eye 8. Skull 9. Ears
10. Cheek 11. Neck 12. Back 13. Tail
14. Loin 15. Thigh 16. Stifle 17. Second
Thigh 18. Hocks 19. Ribbing 20. Elbow
21. Pastern

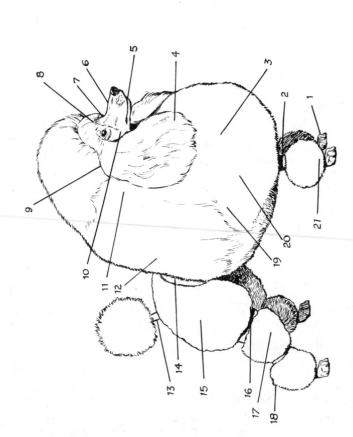

I
A Brief History of the Poodle

Of all the descriptions of the origin of the Poodle which I have seen, I think none surpasses the one contained in the American Kennel Club's publication, "The Complete Dog Book." This begins with the honest admission that the origin of the Poodle is a mystery. That the Poodle was an immensely popular dog in many countries for a great many years is well established.

Many paintings, engravings, bas-relief and pieces of pottery, many by famous artists, through the years, contain likenesses of Poodles as the subject of the paintings or as secondary figures in the paintings and engravings.

Authorities tell us that there is evidence from the Roman civilization, before the birth of Jesus, of jars, dishes, and bas-relief of dogs greatly resembling our Poodle of today, with full front parts and clipped in the hind quarters. There are also samples of bas-relief from the Egyptians in the first century A.D. showing likenesses of clipped Poodles.

Famous painters who have immortalized Poodles on canvas are numerous. Some of the best known are Bernardine Pinturiccio in 1490 who executed a series of paintings featuring Poodles; Gilbert deSeve in the seventeenth century made engravings of the Barbet or Water Spaniel, which looks very much like the Poodle. A painting by Frans Hals between 1584 and 1666 shows a picture of a Toy Poodle attending a garden party. Marlet in 1811 shows a group of dogs at a dog exchange including a large Poodle in "lion clip." Albrecht Durer in the fifteenth century also pictured a toy Poodle in "lion clip" dancing to the music of the flute, played by a small boy. Martin DeVos and the famous Spanish artist Goya both portray Poodles in their paintings. There are many other artists through the years who, in painting pictures of their times, have included Poodles. We are told that the Poodle once, in all probability, was a member of the Spaniel family and this seems to be borne out by descriptions and pictures of the Water Spaniel or "Water Dogge" during the period between 1400 and 1700. The "Water Dogge" or Water Spaniels were used during this period to hunt water fowl. The dog, when possible, actually attacked the game or at least caused the bird to become rattled until his master could arrive and take control. This was not a sport but the deadly serious business of providing food for the table.

It is most probable that these hunters were very particular that their dogs were reliable, intelligent and obedient. It is also probable that if a dog did not meet these requirements he was quickly discarded and replaced by a more desirable one. This may have a great deal to do with the fact that our present day Poodles possess so many desirable characteristics.

White Standard Ch. Alfonco Von der Goldenen Kette, Clairedale and Pennyworth Kennels, owners, Hampton Bays, New York.

The Germans classified their Poodles or *Pudelhund,* as the breed was called, in six classes ·as follows: The *gross* (great) *Pudel,* the *mittlere* (medium) *Pudel,* the *kleine* (little) *Pudel,* the *Schnurl* (corded) *Pudel* and the *Schaf* (sheep) *Pudel. Pudel* in German means "to splash in water."

The French classify their *Caniche* or *Chiencanne* into three classes: Giant or Royal Poodle, which weighs about fifty-five to sixty pounds; the Standard Poodle, which weighs about twenty-five to thirty pounds and the medium or miniature Poodle, which is the smallest. *Caniche* means "little duck" and *chiencanne* means "duck dog."

Around the 1800's the Poodle began to be used less for hunting and more for exhibition at dog shows.

The Poodle Club was formed in 1876, at which time there were two dogs listed in the stud book. Popularity came slowly and in 1881 ten dogs were listed; thirty-three in 1896; one hundred and thirty-one in 1907 and finally in 1908 one hundred and fifty-three were listed. From this point to 1925 popularity fell off until there were only nineteen dogs and bitches registered.

In 1930, due to the interest and support of a small group of persons, the Poodle staged a lively come-back and once again registrations began to climb.

Black Standard Corded, Rejane, Miss Andree Fosset, owner. The cords of a Corded Poodle represent the accumulated previously shed hair which clings to the growing hair.

A few of these hard working persons who did so much to re-popularize the Poodle were Mrs. Byron Rogers, Mr. and Mrs. Sherman Hoyt, Mrs. Whitehouse Walker, Dr. and Mrs. Herbert Sanborn, Mrs. Lee Brady, Mrs. Loring Marshall, Mrs. Hollis Hunnewell, Mr. and Mrs. George Putnam, Mr. and Mrs. Charles Price, and Mr. and Mrs. Justin Greiss. To all of these persons and the many others who have done so much to breed and perpetuate such fine dogs for our amusement and companionship, we owe a great deal. On behalf of Poodle owners everywhere, I say *THANK YOU*.

Today the Toy Poodle is much more a Poodle than he was even a century ago. Then, he was more or less a nondescript small white fluffy dog, as likely as not to be a Maltese Terrier as a true Poodle because the breeds were often crossed. The blue color of the Maltese persists in many even today as the finding of blue puppies unexpectedly in litters of whites crossed with cream-white Toy Poodles verifies.

The so called Classic White Toy Poodle was first crossed with the Miniature in 1940 and only after much discussion did the American Kennel Club recognize crosses between the Toy and the Miniature. It was this crossing which produced the classy little show winning Toys we see today. Before 1940 the Toy was not the dog as moderns know it.

White Toy, Ch. Wilber White Swan, Mrs. Bertha L. Smith, Bethpage, New York, owner. A Best-in-Show Toy.

8

White Miniature, Ch. Adastra Magic Fame, Mrs. Marguerite Tyson, Minden, Nevada, owner.

The crossing, while it changed the form and the color of the old fashioned Toy, brought increased size to the breed so that Toy breeders must be ever alert to breed from the smallest, or there will be pups which grow to the size of Miniatures among the offspring. The Toy is a fairly well fixed breed with only occasional "throwbacks" in size.

Before the standards were fixed in England, France, Germany and in the U.S.A., Poodles of all sizes were to be found spotted with white, or white spotted with colors—parti-colored as such dogs are called. And now today, we occasionally see them again as standards are being changed or relaxed to permit registration of parti-colors again, a fact much lamented by many serious breeders.

The proponents say that a black dog with white feet is a most attractive creature as he stylishly trots along. And who can gainsay them? But will this letting down the bars lead to the production of Poodles with irregular white patches on dark colors or mostly white dogs with "mis-marking of dark colors" as fanciers of other breeds call such color combinations?

Not only is the Poodle a fine retriever and water dog, but he is also a fine actor and trick dog. He has been a companion of royalty as well as the peer. He was once widely used as a truffle hunting dog. Truffles were once a very much sought after delicacy which grows in the ground. Very often Poodles were used in conjunction with a Dachshund, the Poodle finding the location of the truffles and the Dachshund digging them up.

There are a great many stories of Poodles doing unusual deeds, such as the Poodles who were trained to smuggle fine French lace out of Belgium, wrapped around their waists, with a false skin wrapped over the lace. To further prevent detection, these dogs were specially trained to avoid uniformed guards.

The Poodle has ever been the stage trick dog. One sees more Poodles and American Fox Terriers in dog acts than all other breeds combined. Dogs which can be so easily taught, are so eager to please and so responsive that professional trainers use them, can scarcely fail to appeal to those who want superb companions in their homes.

There is one fact about the breed which is not often stressed. One I think is most important to know: Because, over the centuries, every Poodle had to stand and be clipped and groomed several times a year, there has been a wonderful opportunity for selection for the kind of temperament which tolerates kindly this close attention. Except for the terrier breeds which have been plucked, most of the breeds which are clipped today are those so recently treated in this manner that only a few generations have actually been

Black Miniature, Maxine of Rippwood, Mrs. Albert H. Greene, Columbus, Ohio, owner.

White Toy, Ch. Silhou-Jette's Cream Topping. Tom & Ann Stevenson, Challendon Kennels, Salinas, California, owners.

clipped. At first shears, razors and combs were used, later electric clippers. Cocker Spaniels clipping started in 1930 and anyone who has seen the difference in reaction between a modern Cocker the first time it is clipped and a Poodle when it first experiences the sound and feeling of an electric clipper, will realize what I mean.

Over the years Poodles which would not easily tolerate grooming have been eliminated as breeders and those which were natural ladies and gentlemen were more likely to become dams and sires of the next generation. Dogs with such temperaments pleased the owners, and their descendants continue to please Poodle buyers.

From this colorful and interesting past, the Poodle comes to us possessing many of the valuable characteristics for which he has been so highly valued. It is my sincere hope that he will continue on as a breed, unchanged, for many more thousands of years.

Here then are the descriptions of the Poodle types as decided on by the Poodle Clubs. The point scores give the judges the relative importance of the several features of the dog.

Black Toy, Beaujeu Bit-of-Fudge, Mrs. Robert F. Tranchin, Beaujeu Kennels, Dallas, Texas, owner.

TOYS
Description and Standard of Points

(Adopted May, 1938 by The International Toy Poodle Club and Approved by the American Kennel Club, June 14, 1938).

General Appearance. That of a very active, intelligent and elegant looking dog, well built and carrying himself very proudly.

Head. Long, straight and fine, the skull not broad, with a slight peak at the back.

Muzzle. Long (but not snipy) and strong; not full in cheek; teeth white, strong and level; gums black, lips black and not showing lippiness.

Eyes. Almond-shaped, very dark, full of fire and intelligence.

Nose. Black and sharp.

Ears. The leather long and wide, low set on, hanging close to the face.

Neck. Well proportioned and strong, to admit of the head being carried high and with dignity.

Shoulders. Strong and muscular, sloping well to the back.

Chest. Deep and moderately wide.

Back. Short, strong and slightly hollowed, the loins broad and muscular, the ribs well sprung and braced up.

Feet. Rather small, and of good shape, the toes well arched, pads thick and hard.

Legs. Forelegs set straight from shoulder with fine bones and muscle. Hindlegs very muscular and well vent, with the hocks well let down.

Tail. Set on rather high, well carried, never curled or carried over back.

Coat. Very profuse, and of good, hard texture; if corded, hanging in tight, even cords; if non-corded, very thick and strong, of even length, the curls close and thick, without knots or cords.

Colors. Any solid color.

The white, cream, apricot, or red poodle should have dark eyes, black or dark liver nose, lips and toe-nails.

The blue poodle should be of even color, and have dark eyes, lips and toe-nails.

All the other points of Toy Poodles should be the same as the perfect black toy poodle.

N.B. It is strongly recommended that only one-third of the body be clipped or shaved, and that the hair on the forehead be left on.

Size. Toy Poodle—Ten inches or under at the shoulder.

White Toy Ch. Silhou Jette's Snow Sprite, Martha Jane Ablett, Medina, Ohio, owner.

	Points
General appearance and movement	15
Head and ears	15
Neck and shoulders	10
Body, back and tail carriage	25
Color, coat and texture	15
Legs and feet	10
Bone, muscle and condition	10
Total	100

Toy, Ch. Silver Swank of Sassafras, Mrs. Pamela A. P. Ingram, Topanga, California, owner.

STANDARDS AND MINIATURE POODLES
Description and Standard of Points

The following new standard of points for the Poodle, submitted by the Poodle Club of America, has been approved by the Board of Directors of the American Kennel Club, Feb. 14, 1940.

1. *General Appearance, Carriage and Condition.* That of a very active, intelligent smart and elegant-looking dog, squarely built, well proportioned and carrying himself proudly. Properly clipped in the traditional fashion and carefully groomed, the Poodle has about him an air of distinction and dignity peculiar to himself.

14

2. *Head and Expression.*
   (a) *Skull.* Should be slightly full and moderately peaked with a slight stop. Cheek bones and muscles flat. Eyes set far enough apart to indicate ample brain capacity.
   (b) *Eyes.* Oval shape, very dark, full of fire and intelligence.
   (c) *Ears.* Set low and hanging close to the head. The leather long, wide and heavily feathered—when drawn forward almost reaches the nose.

3. *Neck.* Well proportioned, strong and long enough to admit of the head being carried high and with dignity. Skin snug at throat.

4. *Shoulders.* Strong, muscular, angulated at the point of the shoulder and elbow joint sloping well back.

5. *Body.* The chest deep and moderately wide. The ribs well sprung and braced up. The back short, strong and very slightly hollowed, with the loins broad and muscular. (Bitches may be slightly longer in back than dogs.)

6. *Tail.* Set on rather high, docked, and carried gaily. Never curled or carried over the back.

7. *Legs.* The forelegs straight from shoulders with plenty of bone and muscle. Hind legs very muscular, stifles well bent, and hocks well let down. Hindquarters well developed with the second thigh showing both width and muscle.

8. *Feet.* Rather small and of good oval shape. Toes well arched and close, pads thick and hard.

9. *Coat.*
   (a) Quality: *Curly Poodles*—Very profuse, of harsh texture, even length, frizzy or curly, not at all open.
   Corded Poodles—Very thick, hanging in tight, even cords.
   (b) Clip: Clipping either in the traditional "Continental" or "English Saddle" style is correct. In the "Continental" clip the hindquarters are shaved, with pom-poms on hips (optional), and in the "English Saddle" clip, the hindquarters are covered with a short blanket of hair. In both these clips the rest of the body must be left in full coat. The face, feet, legs and tail must be shaved, leaving bracelets on all four legs, and a pom-pom at the end of the tail. The top knot and feathers on the tail must be long and profuse, so as not to lose the very essential Poodle expression. A dog under a year old may be shown with the coat long except the face, feet and base of tail, which should be shaved. Any Poodle clipped in any style other than the above mentioned shall be disqualified from the show ring.

10. *Color.* Any solid color. All but the browns have black noses, lips and eyelids. The browns and apricots may have liver noses and dark amber eyes. In all colors the toe-nails either black or the same color as the dog.

11. *Gait.* A straightforward trot with light springy action. Head and tail carried high.

12. *Size.* The Standard Poodle is fifteen inches or over at the shoulder.

13. *Description and Standard of Points of the Ideal Miniature Poodle.*

(a) Same as Large Poodle.

(b) *Size.* Under fifteen inches at shoulders.

(c) *Value of Points.* Same as Large Poodle.

(d) So long as the dog is definitely a miniature, diminutiveness is only the deciding factor when all other points are equal; soundness and activity are every whit as necessary in a Miniature as they are in a Large Poodle and as these traits can only be seen when the dog is in action, it is imperative that Miniatures be moved in the ring as fully and decidedly as Large Poodles.

POODLE FAULTS
Dish Faced. Too Long in Body. Roached Back. Too Long in Loin. Under Angulated. High in Hock. Shoulders Too Far Forward. Mutton Withers. Shallow in Body.

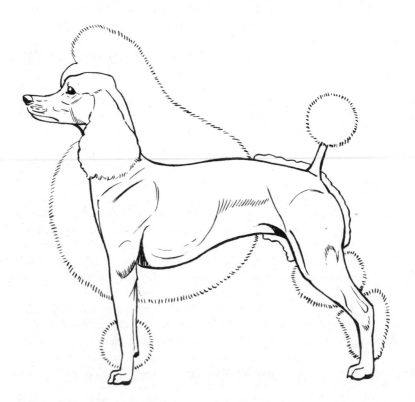

POODLE FAULTS

Wet in Neck. Sway Back, Tail Set Too Low. Over Angulated and Sickle Hocked. Hare Footed. Soft in Pastern. Apple Domed. Short in Neck. Small Boned.

14. *Value of Points.*

	Points
General Appearance, Carriage and Condition	20
Head, Ears, Eyes and Expression	20
Neck and Shoulders	10
Body and Tail	15
Legs and Feet	10
Coat, Color and Texture	15
Gait	10

15. *Major Faults.*

Bad Mouth—either under or over shot.
Cow Hocks.
Flat or spread feet, thin pads.
Very light eyes.
Excessive Shyness.

16. *Disqualifications.*

Parti-colors.
Unorthodox clip.

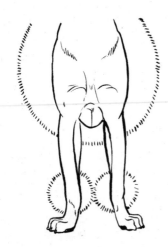
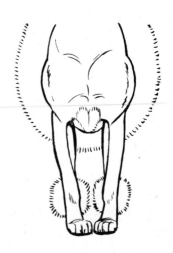

Rear and Front Faults: Upper left—Cow Hocked; Upper Right—Barrel Legged; Lower Left—
Toed Out and Narrow Fronted; Lower Right—Toed In, Shoulders Overloaded.

18

II
Your Dog's Heredity

You may be the owner of a single pet puppy and have not the slightest intention of ever being a breeder. Yet the time will come when you will say, "He's been such a wonderful dog. How I'd like to have one of his own pups to take his place when the dreaded day of parting comes."

You may be alone, or a man and wife who have decided to take up serious dog breeding as a hobby. You may be an established breeder who wants to know what is inherited, and how it occurs. Perhaps you want to learn how to breed out undesirable characteristics which, as we have seen, militate against dogs' popularity, and how to breed in all the brains which those little craniums are capable of holding.

THE GERM PLASM

To get down to basic principles, every dog is the product of the germ plasm which created him and his family. It is carried in the male's testicles and the females's ovaries. Biologically speaking, the only reason for the dog's existence, or our own, is the perpetuation of the germ plasm. So much about natural dogs, and about mankind, is a trick of nature to insure its perpetuation.

Under human direction and management our dogs have become somewhat unnatural, but so have all domestic animals. Man chooses the products of certain germ plasm which best suit his fancy, and since in general these products carry the kind of germ plasm which is likely to produce more of the same kind, man produces what he wants by a process of constant selection.

The educated and experienced dog breeder thinks more about the germ plasm than he does about the individual dogs. He combines this and that, hoping that someday there will be a combination that will produce the dog of his dreams, as nearly as possible like the ideal described by the standard.

This brings us to want to know what it is that makes the changes in different generations—what it is in the germ plasm that controls and creates all the characteristics of individuals.

The mechanism is chemical in nature. Microscopically tiny entities called *genes* which are part of the cell nucleus, are the basic factors. At times of cell division (for any animal is a huge bundle of differentiated cells) the genes arrange themselves into pairs of chains which we call *chromosomes* (color bodies) because they take up certain stains which the rest of the cell does not. When the cell divides into two, one chromosome goes into each daughter cell, splits, and becomes two chromosomes.

Two Outstanding Miniatures. Left: Ch. Tedwin's Two-Step, Ted Young, Jr., Rocky Hill, Connecticut, owner. Right: Ch. Summercourt Square Dancer of Fircot, Mrs. Louis Garlick, Woodmere, New York, owner.

But when the germ cells in the testicles divide to become sperm, only one chromosome of each pair is carried by a sperm. And when the *ova* (eggs) each get ready to unit with a sperm, the egg casts off half of its chromosomes, and, upon combining with the sperm, produces the architectural plans for a new individual. So this new individual inherits half from the germ plasm of each parent.

If you will just remember that *each characteristic of the dog is determined by not one, but two genes in the dog's germ plasm,* it will make it much easier for you to understand this otherwise complicated matter.

Geneticists, the students of heredity, have found that sometimes one gene will be different from its partner in its influence on the production of a given characteristic of the individual. Easiest to explain is coat color, but the principle is the same for many other traits. A dog may have one gene which produces a black coat, and another which produces a mixture of black and white. When the pair work together, the black is able to overpower the parti gene, so the pup this combination produces is black. Therefore such genes are called *dominant;* those overpowered are called *recessive.* If two partis are mated, only partis can result, but if two blacks are mated, each dog having a gene for parti, then some partis might result.

It is all a matter of chance. Here are a pair of genes represented by marbles. The black-producing gene is a black marble, the parti a white marble. Each goes into a separate sperm cell. The dog is mated to a black bitch with the same combination. The chances are the same in her case, so let's represent her genes also by a black and a white marble.

Mix the four marbles in a bowl. Now reach in and take out pairs of marbles. What will you have? You might draw out two blacks, two whites, or a black and a white. The mathematical chances are that from a hundred such tries you would have two blacks 25 times, a black and a white 50 times, and two whites 25 times.

Suppose you mate a black dog, which carries white recessively, with a parti bitch what then? Figure it out: you'll have 50 per cent pure partis and 50 per cent blacks carrying the parti gene recessively, and these of course will be blacks.

So there are six ways, and only six, in which such dogs can be mated.

1. Two pure blacks, which will produce only pure blacks.
2. Two blacks, each of which carries parti genes (hybrid). The expectancy will be 25 per cent pure black, 50 per cent hybrid, and 25 per cent pure parti.

Black Toy Ch. J. C. Lucki Ann, Mrs. H. E. Anderson & Mrs. Jane Fitts, Encore Kennels, Palmetto, Georgia, owners.

21

3. A hybrid black and a pure parti will produce 50 per cent hybrid black and 50 per cent partis.
4. A hybrid black and a pure black will produce 50 per cent hybrids and 50 per cent purebreds.
5. A pure black and a pure parti will produce only hybrids.
6. Two pure partis will produce only partis.

In any single mating these mathematical expectancies may not be realized, but among a hundred matings they would be close. Two blacks have been mated and had a litter of four partis and one black when I expected the reverse, but that does not invalidate the principle, for in the long run my calculations worked out as they should have done.

This principle of dominance and recessiveness in the pairs of genes which determine traits has been studied by many students of canine genetics. It applies to a great many characteristics, not only those of coat color, but of eye color and certain behavior patterns as well.

Then there are other characteristics which are determined by a great many genes. Here is a dog with a perfect gait. Is this dominant over a hitching type of gait? Probably such characteristics are determined by a multiplicity of genes. And the same applies to hunting ability. A poor hunter mated to a good one may produce mediocre workers; the result can't be said to be a

Toy, Bermyth Poodsette Blanche, Mrs. Bertha Smith, Bethpage, New York, owner.

Standard, Gaystream Skyrocket, Mr. & Mrs. Charles R. Miles, Dover, Massachusetts, owners.

genetic certainty. Half a million dollars was spent studying racing ability in horses, but the results simply showed that it pays to mate the best with the best, and that racing ability runs in families; there is no dominance and recessiveness to it, because racing ability represents the development of so many genes that exact prediction is impossible.

OLD IDEAS

In the old days everybody believed that inheritance came about through blood. Many people who ought to know better still speak of pure-blooded dogs, as if blood had something to do with inheritance. A red blood cell is no larger than a dog sperm. Blood gives one a mind picture of dilution, instead of the correct one of presence or absence. Inheritance in dogs is not a matter of mixing of bloods, which would produce blends. We would be better off without such an idea.

Our grandparents thought that a fright experienced by a pregnant bitch would mark her pups; that the effects of one litter carried over to the next; that some of the previous stud's blood stayed around to mix with that of the next stud and ruin the pups. They often killed bitches which had been mismated, because they thought such bitches were ruined for future breeding.

Yes, and they thought acquired characteristics were inherited. Hunt dogs hard and their pups would be better hunters. Practice dogs in standing for shows, and their pups would stand better at shows. Snip off dogs' coats regularly, and their pups would tend to have shorter hair.

These "aids" to breeding are no longer held in respect by geneticists and certainly those who clip dogs know that their dogs' coats sometimes get longer the more generations are clipped. But this is due to selection, and not to clipping at all. This fact alone should disabuse the mind of anyone who entertains any of these old wives' tales.

MUTATIONS

If not by the inheritance of acquired characteristics, how then did all of these amazing differences among dogs come about? How did the very long bushy coat come into existence? How did the increased station (leg length) develop? Where did the various colors come from? They were mutations.

Mutations are sudden changes. Some occur in the germ plasm and breed true. Some are dominant and some recessive. They are exceedingly rare but they do occur and the dog's owner recognizes one and by selective breeding incorporates it as a characteristic.

I have had several mutations which bred true occur in my own dogs. One had a tight screw tail. Leg length is inherited as it is in breed crosses, the shorter legs being dominant over the longer. But imagine my amazement to find an extra short-legged pup among a litter of pups and then to learn by breeding it, that the characteristic was recessive!

Toy Silver, Gregorie's Roulette, Mrs. Betty M. Schmidt, Bethesda, Maryland, owner.

24

Toy, Ch. Cowan's Miel, Mildred C. Bird, Brooklyn, New York, owner.

There was no determiner in the germ plasm of the original stock which could produce the ultra long hair some show winners exhibit. It came by steps, each step being a mutation which was incorporated in a strain by breeding.

Most mutations are downward in the evolutionary scale; only rarely is one an improvement. Many breeders consider the long hair an expression of degeneration just as too short legs are.

INBREEDING (mating between cousins or closer relatives.)

Over and over again owners say to me, in excusing the nasty disposition of their dogs, "Too much inbreeding," or "They're inbreeding these dogs too much these days; spoils their disposition." Obviously some of these evil-tempered dogs are badly trained. Actually inbreeding has very little, if anything, to do with the explanation.

All that inbreeding does is to double up the genes in the germ plasm. If there are desirable genes, it enhances the chances of producing desirable traits; if there are undesirable ones, these, too, come out. Usually it wasn't inbreeding which produces temperaments; it is careless, sloppy breeding. The money breeders don't care what the pups are temperamentally, as long as they *look* as they are supposed to. What does a pet-shop owner usually know about the parents and grandparents of the pups in his window? What does the average puppy buyer demand, beyond the fact that the puppy be cute and cuddly? For a fortnight's playing dolls with a pup, he frequently pays with twelve years' ownership of something which is only obnoxious to anyone who knows dogs.

Judicious inbreeding does not weaken dogs: it fixes traits so they breed true. It makes greater uniformity in a strain. But it does reduce vigor to some extent. Yet after long enough inbreeding, after the undesirable and weakening influences have been eliminated, inbreeding having brought them to light, the animals are all so much alike that they are equivalent to identical twins. There are white rats and mice, used in laboratories, which have been mated brother to sister for more than a hundred generations, and no better laboratory animal can be found.

Standard Puppy, Ostrom's Snow Man, Emil A. Ostrom, Norwood, Massachusetts, owner. This is the clip in which puppies are frequently exhibited.

Miniature Brigadoon's Sabra D'Argette, Dorothy C. Briggs, North Cohasset, Massachusetts, owner.

No one has yet announced the inbreeding of dogs, brother to sister, more than four generations. I tried it with Beagles and the litters became very small, screw tails appeared in several, and by the fourth generation the dogs were smaller than the originals. If one had enough money and enough dogs, the dogs could be bred in this fashion without harm to them, provided that one kept up a rigorous selection. But it is impractical for the ordinary breeder. I cite it to show that not inbreeding, but careless breeding, breeding with no thought of selection, is the reason why we have unreliable dogs.

Line Breeding is simply mating dogs reasonably closely related and keeping within a strain. All the great dog breeders combine line breeding and inbreeding. In fact, one must, to establish a strain. All of our modern breeds were inbred and line bred, as you will find if you study pedigrees.

Out Breeding is mating dogs related only distantly, or, as far as pedigrees show, not at all.

TWINS

There are two kinds of twins in human beings, sheep and cattle; that is, in the species which ordinarily produce but one offspring at a time. Dogs produce litter mates and, rarely, identical twins as do the other species.

Identical twins are enclosed in the same fetal membrane and are quite similar if not identical. Several pair have been born among my dogs and since I first reported a pair of identical puppies in "How to Breed Dogs," several persons have written to me. Some have actually found two pups in one membrane and connected to the same placenta. Such puppies result from the splitting of the newly fertilized egg into two cells each of which develops into a puppy.

So much for some basic principles. Now let us take up the inheritance of some of the individual characteristics that interest all of us breeders.

MENTAL APTITUDES

The simple list of inheritable characteristics known for the Poodle is interesting, but some amplification is necessary. Because behavior patterns are the most important aspects of any dog, we shall consider what is known about mental heredity first.

Miniature Ledahof Brazen Brat, Jerry Silberg, Westfield, New Jersey, owner.

Toy Ch. Most Happy Fella of Woodside, Mrs. Armand Wothe, Butler, Indiana, owner.

Some of the behavioristic school of philosophers tell us there is no such thing as inheritance of mental aptitudes or behavior patterns. But these persons never bother even to glance at what we know about dogs; they work with human beings. But the day of shallowness is passing. One scientist's study of identical human twins upsets all of the claims of non-inheritance made by behaviorists. Yet even this study should not have been necessary to convince the partly-learned psychologists that behavior patterns are just as hereditary as eye color, if in a more complex manner.

The study of the inheritance of trail barking was the first to demonstrate that such behavior is hereditary and independent of training. Dogs of breeds which bay on the trail of game were mated with dogs which trail mutely, and all of the pups barked on the trail. What follows may have no interest to the owner of a pet dog, but will be of considerable interest to a hunter:

Every one of the early "Spaniels" used in cocking "gave tongue" when it scented a bird. For this reason, color in a hunting Spaniel was less important than it is today. You can easily imagine the scene as the early Spaniel was used as an accessory in falconry, the dog busily quartering about in the bush until he scented a bird, then barking as he got closer. A pheasant would run, and the dog would follow him until the bird left the ground.

The hunters would know by the dog's voice that he had "made game" and would remove the falcon's hood. As the quarry shot into the air the incredibly swift falcon would race it and, pouncing down, either injure the bird or catch it in its talons.

If the bird were injured, the Spaniel would retrieve it. Some hunters used to teach their dogs to sit until commanded to retrieve, because if dog, game bird and falcon had met in a free-for-all some damage might well have been expected.

Cocker Spaniels were no exception to trail barking. Indeed we are told that they were bred for a merry tone, and that the tone changed on different kinds

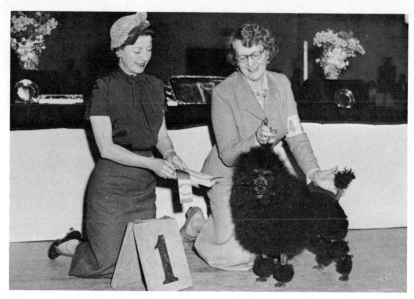

Miniature Twinbark Mistletoe, Mrs. C. Huntlet Chrisman, Twinbark Kennels, Danbury, Connecticut, owner.

of game. This is entirely credible. I can tell from the tone of several of my own hounds whether they have treed a squirrel, a porcupine, a skunk or a 'coon.

Stonehenge, in *On the Dog*, which was published in 1790, says, "*A Spaniel possessing a musical but not noisy voice is all the more valuable if it distinguishes in its notes between the various kinds of game.*" The various kinds of game referred to probably included rabbits. A sight hound must not drop its head to find game but pursue only with its nose, so Spaniels were used to "spring" the rabbits which the Greyhounds, seeing, were "slipped" to chase.

But while most Springer Spaniels today open (give voice) on the trail, Cocker Spaniels do not—on birds, at any rate. I have known them to trail up with Beagles and do a little yipping when they saw a rabbit, but otherwise trail mutely. I have known other Cocker Spaniels which ran on deer trails yipping merrily. Just when the change from open trailing to mute trailing occurred in Cockers we don't know. It must have happened through rigid selection, and Cockers were mostly still or mute trailers as early as 1900. In 1899 we find a comment on a field trial by the association's president, Mr. Arkwright: "*All ran mute with the exception of one puppy.*"

A field trial or hunting bird dog who barks as he hunts, even in recognizing the bird, is practically disqualified. If this characteristic follows inheritance in all other breeds, and it appears to, the open-trailing behavior is dominant over the still trailing. So, once the trait is lost, we should not expect it to show up again from any matings of still trailers. If it is desired, the only way to introduce it is to find a dog that opens on a bird's scent and use him in the matings, inbreeding the progeny until they are pure bred for this individual characteristic.

But this does not mean that the dog will open on all kinds of game. A bird dog that opens on rabbits may not do so on birds. By years of selection, Bloodhounds were developed until they never open on a man trail (training has nothing to do with it), but every one will be wide open on a 'coon or fox trail if he is encouraged to run it.

Standard Ch. Ammsown Gay Knight of Arhill, Mr. & Mrs. Charles E. Wegmann, Ridgefield, Connecticut, owners.

Miniature, Calvinelle Pristine of Trent, Mrs. Calvin B. Hartman, Jr., Silver Spring, Maryland, owner.

Other behavior patterns are clearly inherited, and some not so clearly. I can mention the reaction of puppies to a hypodermic. It is amazing to note how similar the reaction is from one generation to the next. The dogs of some strains stand on the table and take the injections without even wincing. Some pups of other strains brought to the hospital for vaccination will turn their heads and snap at the doctor's hand. This variation in reaction occurs in all breeds of dogs. A Springer breeder brought a station-wagon load of 36 pups for vaccination. All were close to three months old, and in one crate there were five pups of a new breeding which he had recently acquired. All of his own pups stood like rocks when vaccinated, but the five of the strain new to him *all* squealed and urinated.

Among all the bird-hunting breeds, the Spaniels are the only ones which are bred to keep their noses close to the ground, hound fashion, when they hunt. Setters and Pointers hunt with heads high. This is definitely a dominant trait. In crosses made of Cockers with Setters, the puppies all hunted with heads up, like Setters. Even in crosses of Setters with Bloodhounds the progeny were useless as trailing dogs. When you see a Cocker hunt with head carried high, he probably has the genes of the English Setter in him.

The behavior pattern of interest in birds and flying objects, which Setters and Pointers generally show so strongly, is not well developed in some Spaniels. When a butterfly flies through pens containing both Setter and

Cocker pups, the Setters show intense interest, while the Cockers display only a little more interest than hounds of any breed. This indicates that less selection has been applied to the Cocker to make it interested in flying objects, and in this respect the breed is more houndlike, showing a greater degree of interest in ground and body scents.

Perhaps that is why the crosses of Cocker with Beagle make such excellent rabbit and squirrel dogs. Many run almost as well as field trial Beagles, whereas crosses of Beagles and English Setters were worthless in rabbit trailing.

Some of the smaller breeds as well as the larger are natural tree dogs, and many make squirrel dogs *par excellence*, a use to which only those with shorter coats can be put, and to which not enough are put. Some Poodles tree almost as well as tree hounds bred for the purpose, and this aptitude is not so well recognized as it should be, although it is by squirrel hunters. Crossed with American Fox Terriers, the short-haired pups make grand squirrel dogs, illustrating the inheritance of this aptitude.

While most persons never give the aptitude of posing very much thought, observant breeders tell you how much easier it is to get certain dogs to pose as show dogs should than others. There are many who will stand in a show pose when no hand is on or under them. This characteristic quite definitely runs in families.

Toy, Ch. Frosty Boy Carribrook, Lenton W. Sweigart, Denver, Pennsylvania, owner.

33

And there are tremendous differences between the reactions of dogs to an electric clipper the first time one is used on them. No matter how gently a person works, starting on the rear end, stroking dog, talking gently, and taking several times the usual period to perform the task, there are some dogs which are so terrified that they must be anesthetized, in the name of kindness, before the job can be completed. In hospitals and grooming kennels the owners keep special note of the dogs that behave so. Next time they clip them, they may try again to see if they are still panic-stricken. If they are, Pentothal is given again, which the dog enjoys, and he awakens in his new state. Such dogs tend to have the same kind of pups.

Gun-shyness is akin to such temperaments, although occasionally an otherwise temperamentally sound dog may be afraid of loud noises. Gun-shy dogs are invariably thunder-shy. This defect exhibits itself early, and definitely runs in families. At loud reports the dogs really seem to suffer mentally. It is better not to use them for breeding. It is possible to help a gun-shy dog by early training, but such conditioning does not remove the basic defect, and germ plasm which transmits it had better not be perpetuated.

The tendency to piddle is another definitely hereditary weakness which, unfortunately, is generally completely overlooked by breeders. There are many kennels today in which some of the dogs do not wet when approached by strangers, or even by their owners. But there are also too many dogs that

Standard Carillon Fiddle DeDee, Blanche Carlquist, Jacksonville, Florida, owner.

Toy, Ch. Wayne Valley Sir Galahad, Wayne Valley Kennels, Corry, Pennsylvania, owners.

show such incontinence. In a kennel of hunting dogs there is less need to be particular about this defect, but in house dogs it should be diligently watched for and eliminated by selective breeding. That it runs in families none can doubt; that it is a matter of simple inheritance is open to question. Probably this failing is concerned with multiple genes.

Fondness for retrieving shows up in all typical retrieving breeds, including Poodles, yet there are strains that show not the slightest natural interest in it and can be trained only with difficulty. This lack runs in families. To me it is amazing to see a dog whose ancestors have never seen any other birds than English sparrows in a city back yard, who have never had an opportunity to retrieve even one of those sparrows for many generations, yet when the pup is given the chance to do his natural work, he usually acts as if he came from a long line of well-trained hunters. So well does his inheritance persist in him. Still, there are some who, because of so many generations without selection, have lost the hunting ability. Not from the inheritance of disuse, but because of inbreeding of inferior hunters.

So keen is the desire to retrieve in many breeds, to carry something gently in their mouths, that if nothing is accorded them to carry, they may even pick up stools. This sometimes leads to the filthy habit called *coprophagy* (dung eating). It may be corrected many times, by the simple expedient of leaving a few old tennis balls in the runs. The natural retrievers will be found carrying

Standard, Rondelay
Honey Bun, Mrs. S. J.
Fishman, Huntington,
West Virgina, owner.

such tennis balls by the hour. Dog owners sometimes complain that their dogs annoyed them by stealing their shoes, but they really weren't stealing them: *what they were doing was simply trying to satisfy their desire to retrieve.* That is why some dogs learn to "go get things," such as your shoes, on command. Some dogs are more easily taught to fetch your bedroom slippers, bring in the paper, or take the mail from the postman than others. I have even seen a Cocker carry a pound of butter and leave only slight dents in the wrapper. Dogs of most breeds, given such an opportunity, are willing enough to carry the butter, but do so in their stomachs!

Another quite remarkable characteristic of several breeds, Poodles and Cockers especially, used to be manifest in the days when we had great epizootics (animal epidemics) of what was then called *distemper*. When dogs of many breeds have the first rise in temperature which that dreaded disease

Standard, Ch. Putten-
cove Moonshine,
Puttencove Kennels,
Manchester, Massa-
chusetts, owner.

causes they show it by having fits (convulsions). Almost all Beagles had them, yet Cockers, with the same infection, would not. The subsequent mortality was about equal, but the first symptoms are different in some breeds, a fact difficult to explain.

The propensity to want to swim is also hereditary, and markedly so in specialized water-dog retrievers, or even Poodles and Springer Spaniels. There is great variation among them in this regard, and the water-going aptitude is pronounced in a minority. This is one of the reasons why some dogs make so much better house dogs than other retrievers for families who live near bodies of water or even muddy brooks. When dogs of water-going breeds, like Newfoundlands, are crossed with those of non-water-going breeds, the pups are water dogs, showing the dominance of the characteristic. And quite possibly the inheritance is the same in most breeds.

Toy, Inter. Ch. The King's Jester of Encore, Mrs. Jane Fitts, Encore Kennels, Palmetto, Georgia, owner.

COAT CHARACTERISTICS

In the pure-bred dogs of many breeds and in breed crosses we find that the *thickness of the coat* (the number of hairs per inch) tends to be inherited with the thinner coat being dominant. Dogs such as Norwegian Elkhounds, whose coats are extremely dense, when mated to hounds with sparse hair produce houndlike coats. When two of these are mated, about 25 per cent of the pups appear with the dense coats.

In Cockers this holds quite definitely. The woolly-coated dogs often come from parents with proper Cocker coats. This is why it is so easy to breed Woolly Cockers; a pair seldom produces sparse-coated pups.

Wavy hair was dominant over straight hair. The reason dogs have kinky hair or waves in the coat is simply that the guard hair is oval shaped instead of round. This is also the reason why human hair curls.

Length of coat is also inherited, the shorter being dominant, but in all such cases one must realize that color has an effect on hair length. White probably inhibits it; so does red. As I mentioned before, black hair growing in white coats may be many times as long as the white. So the same dog, if it were

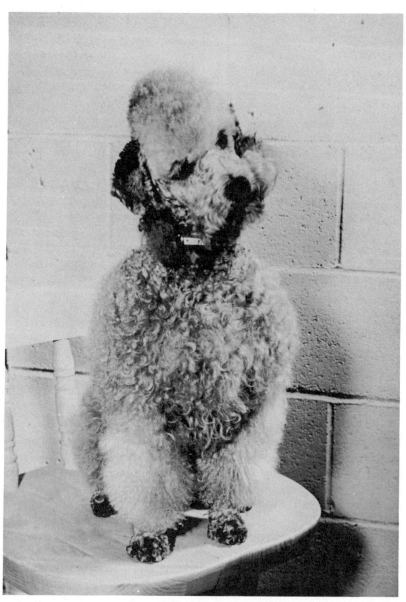

A Silver Miniature in a Dutch Clip.

Miniature, Ch. Braeval Busker, Mrs. J. D. Gant, Chickasaw, Alabama, owner.

black, would have a much longer coat. The very long haired Corded Poodle's coat is recessive to the medium length coat, we may surmise, although no studies have been reported. But since Poodles with normal coats have been known to produce pups whose hair "grew in long strings," it is reasonable to assume the long hair is recessive.

This, then, is not a simple matter of inheritance. Coat length seems to be inherited, with the shorter coat in each degree being dominant over the longer. If an American Fox Terrier were mated with the Poodle with the longest, most woolly coat, the pups would have short, smooth coats. If a pure, medium-length coated Poodle were mated to the extreme type, the pups would have medium-length coats. This obtains if the dogs are all of the same color.

How about coarseness of coat? Here again we find the coarser dominant over the finer. It occurs when different strains are crossed within the breeds of Poodles, and this again explains why it is so easy to breed fine-textured woolly coats.

III
Poodle Colors and their Inheritance

It is astonishing how few persons know that Poodles appear in any other colors than black, brown and white. Some few know about apricot and greys but, outside of the realm of serious Poodle breeders, breeders of large numbers of the several types, the knowledge of Mr. and Mrs. Public is far too limited in this respect.

In Continental Europe only blacks, browns and white are eligible for registration. In England other colors may be registered. In America, some Poodle breeders tell us that Poodles come in more colors than dogs of any other breeds. Let's see. What are these many colors?

Miniature, Ch. Ledahof Silverlaine, Mrs. E. A. Dalton, Ledahof Kennels, New Brunswick, New Jersey, owner.

Miniature Toy, Nibrock Pixie, Byron W. Elder, Renea Toy Poodles, Pitcairn, Pennsylvania,

Black, Mahogany black
White, clear
White in appearance, but actually silver
White with cream tinge
White, born black which changed to apricot, then white
Apricot
Apricot, born black, usually carrying black or grey hairs on the ears
Apricot, born rusty black, usually carrying black or grey hairs on the
    ears
Cream, also called *ivory* and *cream white*
Cream, born black
Silver
Silver, born black
Platinum, born silver
Chinchilla
Black-and-tan
Blue
Brown with black noses and foot pads
Brown with red noses and foot pads and yellow eyes
Any of the above spotted with white

To understand coat color inheritance in Poodles, one must take into account what geneticists call formulas. Each gene is given a name and the name is simply one or more initials. *B* stands for black. Other genes act only, so far as can be determined, to modify color in which case their letter or letters are written above and to the right of the B, just as the square of a number is written 6^2. Or the modifying gene insignia may be written on the same line. Brown Poodles with brown noses, foot pads and yellow eyes are blacks with a pair of inhibiting genes which prevent the full expression of the black.

Few persons understand that dog hair is packed with granules of color which are what gives a dog the color we see. The genes which control color affect these color granules. There is even recognized, a greying gene which causes fading or gradual loss of color as the dog ages.

A typical formula of a black Poodle might be $A^sA^sBBCCDDEEGGSS$. Or the dog could still be a black with this formula $A^sa^tBbCcDdEeGgSs$.

The symbols at present accepted by serious geneticists for the coat colors are as follows:

A^s	—	Colored all over (self colored)
A^t	—	Black and tan pattern
B	—	Black
b	—	Inhibited black (brown)
C	—	Colored
c	—	Albino, no pigment in hair or eyes
C^{ch}	—	Chinchilla (cream)
D	—	Intense pigmentation
d	—	Dilution, changing black to blue, brown to pale brown
E	—	Extension of pigment in hairs
e	—	Restriction of pigment, producing apricot and cream
G	—	Greying which changes colors to grey or silver
g	—	Absence of greying factor
S	—	Unspotted
s^2	—	Some small spots of white
s^w	—	Extreme spotting producing almost a white dog

Now you may ask, "How are these characteristics inherited?" When you see a capital letter you know it is dominant. The appearance of any dog gives one a small idea of his or her genetic formula but, you ask, "How do I know the complete formula of my dog?" The only way is by breeding it to dogs of many colors in the opposite sex and noting the results. Knowing the color of the dog's parents often provides a clue. Thus, should your dog be a black which was produced from the mating of a clear white dog and a cream or ivory (this has happened) you would know your dog was capable of producing quite a wide variety of colors.

Those interested in pursuing the study of Poodle coat color seriously should read Dr. C. C. Little's *The Inheritance of Coat Color in Dogs;* Dr. David D. Whitney's excellent monographs; and a fine concise treatise on The White Toy Poodle by Mrs. C. C. Potter. The latter two have carried Dr. Little's study forward and have added to our knowledge materially. All deserve great credit for their scientific devotion to the work.

You already know enough about the way dominant and recessive characters behave in heredity so that you can figure the chances of any mating if you know the genetic constitution of any pair of dogs; whether they carry recessive or dominant genes for a given coat color. So it should be a simple matter to make fairly accurate prognostications. But as was previously mentioned, only when you know what the pair of dogs carry recessively.

Recent papers of Dr. David D. Whitney's dealing with the puzzling cases of (1) white, (2) apricot, and (3) black-born apricot Poodles are published herewith because they help, more than any study, to clarify this question. Actually, as you will see, the papers deal with several colors and the results of practical kennel matings.

A beautiful White Toy Poodle.

WHITE POODLES

by David D. Whitney   University of Nebraska

Well-groomed white Poodles, with the contrasting colors of their jet-black noses and white coats have been popular in some of the European countries for a long time and are beginning to be favorites in some sections of this country. There are two kinds: the ivory-whites with a few apricot-colored hairs in their coats, indicating that they would have been apricots if they had not been white; and the snow-whites or ice-whites with a few black hairs in their coats, indicating that they would have been black dogs if they had not been white. Their white color is caused by the activity of a pair of recessive genes, the extremely white piebald genes which prevent the formation of pigment in the hairs.

Spotting

Many amateur Poodle breeders consider themselves fortunate in having selected solid-colored breeding stocks with which to start their kennels. They even may boast of their solid-colored puppies but, after a while, one of their puppies may be born with small white spots on its chest. Its appearance seems a mystery and immediate resolutions are made to destroy it with the hope that there will be no more born like it. Such hopes are seldom realized!

The white spots are the result of the activities of recessive genes which have been in the stock in an inactive state, perhaps for many generations, until in the present mating, when two of them have been inherited by the puppy, one from each parent, forming a pair which at once begin to prevent the formation of pigment in the hair of small areas on the chest. The other puppies in the litter were lucky in not receiving a pair of these genes, but probably received one which they may pass on to their offspring for making white spots in later generations.

Some of the dogs in other breeds, as Fox Terriers, Collies, Pointers, Cocker Spaniels and others, have larger white areas or spots in their coats due to another pair of recessive, depigmenting genes. In the white Bull Terrier the white area is so large as to nearly cover the whole coat (sometimes it does), leaving only a black spot of color on the head or ear. A third pair of recessive, depigmenting genes, the extremely white piebald genes, cause the large white area to further increase in size so as to actually cover the entire dog, but leaving a few traces of the original coat color in a few of the hairs, as in many of the white dogs of other breeds. The nose, eyes, lips and footpads are not affected but retain their original black color.

Ivory-white Poodles

The white Poodles having traces of apricot colors easily may be identified by placing either the dog or a generous sample of its hair against a white background of paper or cloth. The ivory tints will be evident at once. There is considerable variation in the extent and depth of the apricot coloring in the coats. Sometimes it may be a conspicuous biscuit coloring on the ears or even throughout the entire coat, but in others the traces are practically unnoticeable to an ordinary observer. Some people state that there also may be pink tints in the coats of some dogs. In many coats the apricot hairs may be readily seen in direct sunlight or by using a reading glass or in microscopic preparations of hair samples.

Snow-white Poodles

The white Poodles having traces of black hair easily may be identified as ivory-whites by placing them against a white background. No ivory tints will be seen but their coats will be a cold-white color. Some dogs, however have more traces of black in their coats than others, and may appear slightly grayish in places or throughout their entire coats. An examination of the coats in strong sunlight usually will show a few black hairs, or by using a hand lens, or by observing prepared samples of the hair under a microscope.

Puppies

As the genes for white are recessive, a pair of white Poodles always produce white puppies, which may appear whiter than their parents, owing to more enclosed minute air globules in their hairs than in adult dogs. When the puppies mature, very few of their new, small fur hairs contain air globules, resulting in a diminishing of the intense whiteness in their adult coats.

A pair of ivory-whites will produce ivory-white puppies. A mating of an ivory-white, with an apricot-colored dog will produce all apricot-colored puppies in various shades of apricot, which are likely to fade readily in the sunlight.

Toy, Ch. Nibroc Vivian, Mrs. Clement K. Corbin, Summit, N. J., owner.

Fashions in Poodles. Sweaters made to match those of the owners.

A pair of snow-white dogs may produce either snow-white or ivory-white puppies, depending on whether or not they carry apricot genes in their underlying black color.

The submerged black and apricot in the white dogs may carry as many recessive-color genes as any ordinary black or apricot dog. No one can predict with any assurance, what the colors of puppies will be when one parent is white and the other one colored, except in the mating of an ivory-white and an apricot. Two white dogs mated to colored ones have been reported to have produced not only black, apricot and white but also brown and silver puppies. Blue and the undesirable black-and-tan genes may be carried by apricots and blacks, so no one should be surprised to see these colors appear from the matings of some of the whites with colored dogs.

As all the genes for the various kinds of white spotting are recessive, a single one of these genes may be carried in a dormant state for many generations in solid-colored Poodles. But when it meets another similar gene in a puppy, white areas are developed in the coat. It was reported some years ago, that after 19 successive generations of black breeding, a pure white (extreme white piebald) puppy was born in a litter of black puppies. At that time it seemed unexplainable, but with the present knowledge of the laws of inheritance, such a sudden appearance of a white puppy is no longer mysterious.

Standard, Tambarine de La Fontaine, Alekai Kennels, Mr. & Mrs. Henry J. Kaiser, Honolulu, Hawaii, owners.

APRICOT POODLES

There are differences of opinion concerning the color of apricot Poodles. Some dog fanciers speak of them as being of yellow-orange-tan shades, ranging from pale cream to a very light russet color, with black noses; others say that they should have the color of a ripe apricot, with black noses.

Black-nosed Apricots

The black-nosed apricots have dominant genes for black which begin to develop black pigment in the skin and hair of the unborn puppies, but their influence is soon counteracted by another set of genes, the apricot genes, that change the black pigment to a red-tinted apricot color. The puppies are born with apricot coats; have black noses and bluish skins.

In addition to the genes for black and apricot, there may be a third set of genes which may begin to function to cause the apricot-colored pigment to change to pale shades of cream, called *chamois* by the English. When these three sets of genes are present some of the puppies of a litter may be born dark or light apricots, and others dark or light creams. (It is often impossible to distinguish the light apricots from the dark creams). All of the puppies, apricots and creams, have black noses and are considered by many fanciers to be the true apricots and creams. Pure lines of black-nosed apricots and creams always produce the coat and nose colors of their parents. Kennel reports have been received of eight litters by black-nosed parents, four sires and five dams, totaling 34 black-nosed apricot and cream puppies.

Apricots May Carry Inactive Genes for Other Colors

Some English breeders have bred their pale apricots and creams to dogs of other colors in an attempt to darken their color. As black is a foundation color in apricots and creams it can take on recessive genes of other colors and carry them indefinitely in an inactive state. When, however, one of these inactive genes is passed on to a puppy by its sire, and its recessive mate is passed on by the dam, then, these genes form a pair and become active in producing their own particular color in the puppy.

Toy, Encore Silver Showman, Encore Poodles, Mrs. Jane Fitts, Palmetto, Georgia, owner.

Toy, Ch. Chocolate Bud de Bur Mar, Encore Poodles, Mrs. Jane Fitts, Palmetto, Ga., owner.

Brown Inactive Genes in Apricots

Any breeder may acquire perfect-colored, black-nosed apricots and later be astonished to see in the first litter some brown-nosed puppies with the black-nosed ones. Both, however, have the apricot genes, but in the black-nosed puppies they have been causing a change of color of the black pigment; whereas, in the brown-nosed puppies they have been causing a change of the color of the brown pigment, producing slightly different colors. Superficially, the two coats may appear to be alike but a careful scrutiny will show that those of the black-nosed puppies will have pink tints, giving them warmer tones; and those of the brown-nosed puppies will lack pink tints in their dull-brownish coats. A few kennel records show: that five litters, by two black-nosed cream sires and three similar dams, contained 19 puppies, 12 with black noses and 7 with brown noses. Brown-nosed Poodles breed true and never produce black-nosed puppies.

Black-and-Tan Inactive Genes in Apricots

A fancier may be more surprised when his black-nosed apricot or cream sire and dam produce a litter in which one or two of the puppies are the ordinary black-nosed apricots and creams, but the other three or four are very dark, reddish black and tan coloring on the feet, undersides of the body, over the eyes and perhaps in other places, a modified black-and-tan pattern. The dark parts of the coats are made up of a mixture of black and reddish-black hairs in the ratio of about 1:3. Soon after birth, however, the roots and bases of the dark hairs begin to become apricot or cream coats, but with many intermingled black-guard hairs. In the following months the black hairs are shed and uniform apricot or cream coats are finally completed. Records of two litters, by two sires and two dams, have been received, having eight puppies, three creams and five dark-reddish blacks, having the black-and-tan patterns. All had black noses. The darkest ones which were allowed to live were changing to apricot colors at 12 weeks, much to the surprise of the owners.

Berrydale's Brown Poodles in Smart Collars. Mother & Son.

Silver Inactive Genes in Apricots

The foundation color in silvers is also black but the apricot genes can change the black pigment in a silver to an apricot or cream color before the birth of the puppy so one does not suspect that the dog is a carrier of silver genes until proper matings are later made. One kennel reports a litter by a black-nosed cream sire and a blue dam. Of the four puppies born black, two of them cleared to silver. *A gene for silver must be contributed by each parent for the production of a silver puppy.*

The Overpowering Apricot Genes

Some people might consider the dominant black pigment genes as the most influential ones, as they can associate with one or more of the recessive color genes and prevent them from functioning. As the effects of a pair of apricot genes on other colors are studied, one is reminded of the ancient alchemist whose highest hopes (never realized) were to be able to change all metals into gold. When the apricot genes become associated with a sparkling black they at once transform it into a golden apricot with pink tints; a somber brown is readily changed to lovely honey and cream colors but without the pink tints; the least desirable color of black-and-tan is more resistant to changes, but it is overcome and develops into a typical apricot color; and a gleaming silver is easily transformed into a delicate cream. There are, however, many variations of color shades in these transformations but their end results are always in apricots and cream shades.

Silver Miniature Poodle "Ch. Salute of Ledahof" owned by Miss Elizabeth Van Sciver, Malvern, Pa.

Silver Toy Poodle "Ariane's Petit Zee Zee" owned by Muriel and Richard Hucknall, North Hills, N. Y.

Black-nosed-White, Apricot and Cream Matings

Some of the ordinary white Standard and Miniature Poodles are often considered the last stages of color reduction in creams, retaining only their black noses and possibly a few hairs on the ears that are slightly tinged with cream. Theoretically, when such whites are mated with apricots and creams, all of their puppies should be born apricots or creams, as both parents belong in the same color group. One kennel reports a litter of 11 black-nosed apricot and cream puppies, by a Standard black-nosed dark apricot sire, one puppy was as dark as the sire. Other kennels report five litters totaling 3 apricot puppies and 20 cream puppies, by three Miniature apricot and cream sires and four Miniature white dams, all dams, sires and puppies with black noses.

As the genetic background of some of the white Toy Poodles and many of the other white Miniatures and Standards are different from those of the extremely diluted apricot Standards and Miniatures, their offspring, by apricots and creams, may be black or of other colors.

Summary

The apricot genes change the color of the black pigment in the coats of black-nosed black, black-and-tan, silver and probably blue Poodles to various reddish-orange shades; and the color of the brown pigment in the brown-nosed Poodles to various shades of delicate browns, honey colors and cream puppies.

Acknowledgements for breeding records and hair samples are made to the following kennels: Nikolane, Orchard House, Sherwood Hall and Welchacre.

Perhaps you feel now, as so many other Poodle owners and breeders do, that all Poodle registrations should not only tell the dog's color but should carry the additional information telling the color the dog was at birth. This would be a great help to serious breeders. If the kennel clubs which register Poodles could not arrange room on their certificates, surely every pedigree blank, private or official, should carry the information.

IV
Inheritance of Poodle Size

While it is true that dogs of the Standard size Poodle are quite uniform, it is also true that dogs of the Miniature and Toy sizes are anything but uniform. This, as we have seen is due to the crossing of the types, especially during the past fifty years.

To a certain extent Standards produce puppies too small to be Standards and too large to be Miniatures, a fact also attributable to type crossing. Nor is it unusual to find that miniatures have occasional puppies too large for their class and too small to be good Standards.

It is in the Toys and Miniatures where we find most of the departures from their proper sizes. Poodle breeders have tried to explain size inheritance too simply.

Geneticists talk about *Pure Lines* and Poodle size inheritance is a very good illustration of the principle. After a group of animals has been bred for many years they become more and more uniform. Considering their size, we would find that there was some variation, of course. We should find that when we mated those at the largest end of the scale, the offspring would seldom be larger than the largest representatives and that the progeny would vary around the upper end of the scale with none down to the small end.

Conversely, when we mated a pair of the smallest, their young would all tend to be small and few if any be as large as those at the large end of the scale. Each of these groups would be pure lines.

Now when an animal from the largest size is crossed with one from the smallest size the progeny will vary from large to small. It will take many generations to breed them into pure lines again. And this is the case with Poodles today. It accounts for the variation we find.

At one time the Toys, even though they were Maltese Terrierish, constituted more or less, a pure line. So did the Miniatures and the Standards. Came the crossing of the types and the germ plasm which is responsible becomes scrambled with genes for several sizes. As a consequence, it will take many generations to breed them into pure lines again. And until they are fixed by selective breeding, we can continue to expect Poodles of all three types to occasionally produce off-sizes.

Even within well established strains there is variation as there is in all breeds. Those who want the tiniest possible Toys must continue to breed from the smallest. Many generations of breeding for size does fix a strain size so there is little variation.

From the point of view of a person interested in buying a Poodle with the expectation it will not grow to be too large or too small, the best advice one can give is to urge the prospective purchaser to observe all of the closely related representatives to see how large they grew. It is usually safe to trust the word of the breeder who can describe the near kin. If there is variation within a family of Poodles, and if one wants a small one, it is generally safe to choose the smallest in the litter. Rarely does the smallest overtake the larger as they grow, although it has been known to happen.

This principle is especially valuable to understand particularly for those breeding Toys which like other midget breeds tend to have very small litters; some producing only one or two puppies at a time. If a bitch is to be selected from a pure line of Toys which always produce small progeny, the sensible thing is to choose the largest of that pure line, knowing that her puppies will tend when mature, to be smaller than their mother. Breeding her to a small stud of excellent type and from a strain known to produce several puppies per litter should insure a fair sized litter.

It is well known that the more puppies in a litter the smaller they average to be and the less likelihood of the need for a Caesarian operation. Toy bitches which produce only one puppy seem to be much more in need of surgical assistance than those which produce three or four.

White Standard pup, Danbe's Pepe La Moke, Mr. & Mrs. Dan Noonan, owners.

Toy, Merrymorn Lita, Mrs. Milton Erlanger, New York, New York, owner.

There is, most likely, a tendency for some strains to whelp larger litters, just as there is in the case of all other species including human beings to have multiple births. Apparently no studies of the tendency have been made in midget dogs, but among the larger breeds common observation indicates that there are strains within breeds, and especially mongrels which are much more prolific than others. One huge St. Bernard bitch gave birth to 41 puppies in two litters. One of her daughters produced 19 puppies twice. A 60 lb. mongrel produced three litters of 18 puppies each. A Beagle weighing 19 lbs. produced 11, 13, 12 and 9 puppies in four litters.

One Toy Poodle has produced litters of 6, 7 and 6 puppies consecutively. She is on the large side, but not too large to show.

A Toy Poodle in a Mink cape, held by his owner, Mrs. Rosemary DeCamp, Television Star.

V
Reproduction in the Bitch

In order to be a fairly successful breeder it is not essential that you understand the processes of reproduction. You can proceed by hit-or-miss, by reliance upon tradition, which stems from a conglomeration of old wives' tales and general attempts to explain phenomena without the underlying knowledge we have today. Or you can leave it all to your veterinarian; but that will be unnecessarily expensive.

One of the most attractive features of dog breeding is the fact that those who get the most out of it are those who travel down the bypaths into which it leads them in search of knowledge. There are so many of these temptations, and they are all intriguing. Reproduction is one of the most rewarding and fascinating of them. Many people who know very little about human reproduction have considerable information about canine, and of course they catch the implications. Many parents find that letting their children learn about reproduction from watching the phenomenon in dogs, and helping with a few bits of information as the children acquire knowledge, is one of the finest ways of dealing with the matter. Our children learned in that way. We explained, when they asked, about the inside happenings, ovulation, gestation,

Poodles make wonderful, loyal companions.

and so forth, and they never did ask the silly questions so often put by children who acquire their information on street corners, or behind the barn, from other children.

Despite today's broad education, the public know practically nothing about their own reproduction, and what they think they know is mostly erroneous, so how can they be expected to understand it in dogs ? I have often asked women clients, to whom I am about to explain the "facts of life" about their bitches, if they know what day of the cycle the human female ovulates. Surely 95 per cent of them never heard the word, judging by their expression of bewilderment.

Probably this is all "old hat" to you; if so, skip it. If not, read it, because if you are a serious dog breeder it may save you time and money.

The female ovaries, that part of her for which all the rest of her exists, are located inside her abdomen, high up and just behind her last ribs. They are about as large as a yellow-eye bean but a little more compressed (flatter). Each ovary is encircled by a capsule, in one side of which there is a slit, with spongy tissues along its edge, called fimbria. Starting from this tissue, a tiny

A pair of imported youngsters in puppy coats. Puckshill Amber Flare & Puckshill Amber Fascinator. Keegan Kennels, A. H. Martin, Saco, Maine, owner.

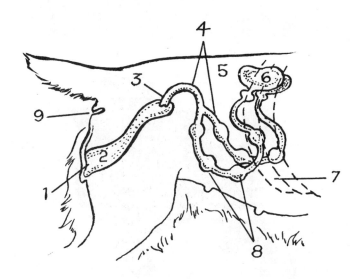

Female organs of reproduction. Reproductive system of a bitch. (1) Vulva. (2) Vagina. (3) Cervix. (4) Uterus. (5) Ovary. (6) Kidney. (7) Location of ribs. (8) Lump consisting of embryo and placenta. (9) Anus.

tube runs in a zigzag course over each capsule and terminates at the upper end of one of the branches of the uterus (womb). These tubes are called Fallopian. The uterus is constructed in the shape of a letter Y. The illustration shows the difference in anatomical construction between the human and canine reproductive tracts. It is considerable. Many of those persons who have some knowledge of the human tract think the long arms of the uterus in the bitch are Fallopian tubes, but such is not the case.

When a bitch becomes pregnant, the fertilized eggs nest at various places along the uterus, which expands to accommodate their growth and to protect them as well. A bitch with a dozen pups in her uterus will have developed each of its horns to perhaps thirty inches long and two inches in diameter.

When *copulation* (the mating of dog with bitch) occurs, sperm are transferred and are moved up the uterus by the same sort of movement (peristalsis) that occurs in the intestines. Within a few minutes after tieing (sexual fusion) occurs, the sperm are already up the uterus, through the Fallopian tubes, and in the capsule surrounding the ovaries.

Black Miniature, Denbur's Another New Hat, Mrs. G. M. Caskey, Jr., Gran Ellen Kennels, Athens, Georgia, owner.

THE MATING CYCLE

Within the ovaries of the bitch there is a rhythmical period transpiring, very much like the human. But while the average human female has thirteen periods in a year, the chief difference in canines is that only two of these periods come to full development during a year. It is interesting to know why.

The changing length of the day is apparently the chief influence in inducing a cycle which brings the female reproductive tract into a condition where she will, during part of it, "accept the dog." As the days grow longer in the latter part of winter, and when they get noticeably shorter in late summer, the vast majority of bitches come into heat.

This fact can be used to bring a bitch into heat. If the length of her day is increased by artificial light, one hour a day for the first week, two hours the second, three the third, and four the fourth, she will usually be in heat. Or shipping a bitch from, say, the vicinity of Boston to some city in Georgia will usually accomplish the same result in less than six weeks. The reverse produces the same effect, especially when it is done during the winter when days are short, and provided the bitch is not kept in a lighted kennel or in your home.

The germ plasm stored in the ovaries, ripens eggs which develop in blister-like pockets that grow toward the surface of the ovaries. Of these there are a great many more than there are eggs which become puppies. At a certain time, about the fourteenth to sixteenth day (much as is the case with the human female), these pockets, called follicles, are as large as small peas, and protrude from the bean-shaped ovary. The follicles produce *follicular hormone*, which acts to prepare the uterus. When they cannot stand the internal pressure any longer, due to the thinning of their walls, most of the follicles which have protruded from the ovary burst and liberate the eggs (ova) into the capsule around it.

They are beset by a multitude of male sperm, provided, of course, the bitch has just been bred. It was formerly thought that one sperm was sufficient to penetrate an egg, but we now know that a large number of sperm are required to break down the egg's resistance, because the sperm have an enzyme which weakens the egg's coating, and then one sperm can get through.

The eggs, whether fertilized or not, are moved through the Fallopian tubes down into the uterus and there, if they have been fertilized, they become attached to the uterine lining (endometrium) and grow. If they have not

Black Miniature, Forest Mister Black, Dr. Ralph A. Logan & Edward Jennings, Libertyville, Illinois, owners.

joined with sperm already, they may meet them in their downward passage and, becoming fertilized, nest in the uterus.

Since ovulation does not occur before the middle of the acceptance period (which starts at the eighth or ninth day from the first showing of swelling of the vulva and bleeding), the ideal time to mate dogs is close to ovulation, either a day before, or any time during the rest of the period. The fragile sperm do not live more than three days in the female tract, and perhaps are not able to fertilize when they are more than two. This is the reason why bitches mated the first day they will take the dog so often fail to become pregnant: the sperm cannot live until the eggs have been discharged from their follicles.

As soon as the follicles rupture, the pits made by this phenomenon fill with blood, thus forming bloody plugs called the blood bodies (corpora hemorrhagica). These soon change their characteristics and secrete a hormone, the luteal hormone, whose effect is almost opposite from that of the follicular hormone. The blood bodies become quite tough and, since they take up yellow stain when prepared for study, are called the luteal bodies. These corpora lutea persist during pregnancy and for some time thereafter.

The luteal hormone puts the brakes on the whole mating cycle. Shortly after the luteal hormone enters the blood stream, the bitch's vulva, which has

Black Miniature, Ch. Poodhall Gus, Poodhall Kennels, Caistor Centre, Ontario, Can., owners.

White Miniature, Midcrest Ice-A-Rama, Miss D. Valerie Reid, Doral, P.Q., Canada, owner.

become firm and greatly swollen, loses its firmness, and within 36 hours becomes flabby and soft. If you own a bitch but have failed to note her first day, perhaps even being appraised of her condition by the action of your male dogs or of neighbors' dogs camping on your lawn, then watch for this sudden softening of the vulva. It means she has ovulated, and that you had better not delay many days before mating her.

When she has conceived, in other words when the male sperm and eggs have joined and a new pup has been started, the egg with its complete pairs of chromosomes divides into two. Each of the daughter cells formed from the fertilized egg has complete pairs of chromosomes. This process of cell division continues until about the sixth, when one pair of cells is set apart to become the germ plasm of the pup.

The dividing cells become a hollow globe, which finally pulls in one side, just as if you let the air out of a hollow rubber ball and pushed one side of it in until it touched the other side, then squeezed it together until you made a canoe-shaped body, squeezing further until the two gunwales of the canoe touched and stayed together. What was the outside of the ball is now its inside.

This new formation grows and grows by cell division, until by the twenty-second day it is a very tiny object surrounded by protective coverings and the

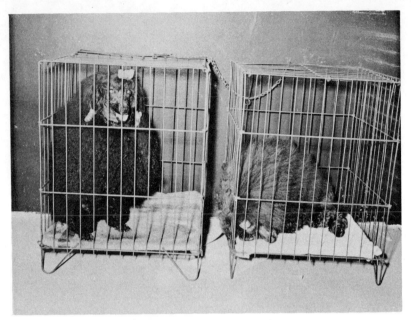

Poodles in cage at Westminster show.

placenta, which connects it to the uterus. If you have a delicate sense of touch, you can feel it through the abdominal wall. You must put your thumb on one side of the bitch's belly, your fingers on the other side, and, feeling very gently, you will discover several lumps. They feel like tiny marbles, round and uniform.

By the twenty-fourth day they will be noticeably larger, and every day they will grow larger until the thirty-fifth day. After that the lumps will be so soft that they will be difficult to feel, but one scarcely needs to anyway, because the size of the belly is a good indication.

If your bitch ovulates and does not conceive because she was not bred, the stud was sterile, or the mating took place too early, she will develop enlarged breasts, an increased appetite, and, 60 to 63 days from the time she ovulated, will go through most of the activity of a bitch about to whelp, yet not produce pups. She may steal other pups to mother; she may produce some milk, so don't think she is sick. Rather, if she does not do these things, consider the probability that she did not ovulate. She will not retain the *corpora lutea* and may come into heat two months earlier than you expect.

In the days when Carre's disease was the great scourge of dogs it was very common to find bitches pregnant at the time they contracted the disease resorbing their puppies. I reported this fact many years ago in a veterinary journal. The interesting thing was that when the bitch did this, the pregnancy protected them against the disease so that its effects were so mild one often would not normally know they were sick. This accounted for the survival of many more bitches than dogs in epizootics of that horrible disease.

Have you ever listened to discussions among dog breeders on whether to breed a bitch on her first, second, or third heat? If not, then if you are at all scientifically minded, get such an argument started and sit back and listen. I have done it, many times, to learn all the ideas dog breeders have. In every such discussion the ideas most often expressed are based on thoughts about human beings. An adroit *why* interjected here and there soon brings out the fact that nearly all of the ideas are also based on rationalization and not knowledge. Here are some:

"You wouldn't want to see a thirteen-year-old girl have a baby, would you? Answer: a thirteen-year-old girl is not grown or physically mature when she first menstruates; a bitch doesn't come in heat until she is mature. Time of marriage is a social convention. Moreover, a woman obstetrician tells us that the thirteen-year-old girls she has delivered have had their babies much more easily than older women.

"Puppies from older bitches will be better puppies than those from young

Black Toy, Ch. J. C. Midnight Madman, Eileen M. Slyder, Dayton, Ohio, owner.

ones." Anyone who makes this claim should present evidence, and all scientific studies show it to be without foundation. Many champions have come from bitches bred their first heats. Those who support the view with arguments should realize that they are also supporting the argument for the inheritance of acquired characteristics, a viewpoint pretty well vitiated by research. It is probably true that one can find more champions from the second heats of bitches than from the first, but this is because many breeders skip breeding the first heat through mistaken notions.

"A bitch isn't old enough to take proper care of puppies before she is two years old." More rationalizing. True, she may take better care of her second litter because of experience, but that is a very different matter. Mother love in a bitch is based on hormone production (prolactin). The second litter is no longer novel to her. She may take better care of her fourth. On the basis of the above argument she should never have her first litter.

The scientifically minded dog breeder wants to know why, and when he inquires of those with experience, he learns that many breeders have found (that a bitch bred her first litter) may have better spring of ribs than one bred later, because while her bones are "less brittle" they are pushed outward and tend to "set that way." How much of fact or fancy there is in this idea we do not know from research, but it is the opinion among a wide segment of fanciers who breed their bitches the first heat on this account, and find it does them no harm.

Four Cuties of Highland Sand & Braeval Strains. Raised by Keegan Kennels, Saco, Maine,

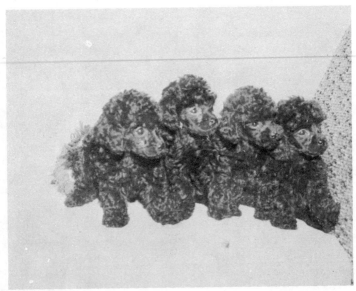

Black Miniature, Arcady Black Jack, Gloria C. Berlin, & Mrs. Robert Wellens, Walnut Creek, California, owners.

The person with an open mind also asks those who, like myself, have bred dogs in studies, and learns that we always breed the first heat and have had no bad results.

Then there is another point too often overlooked, namely the possible loss of unique, valuable germ plasm which a puppy may carry. Dogs are subject to so many perils that their average age is probably not over five, and it is best to have litters as early as possible to be sure of getting any.

Besides, where space is limited it pays a breeder to know what kind of puppies a dog produces, so he can keep the best producers and eliminate the inferior. Why keep a bitch an extra year to find this out?

Many breeders owning valuable bitches have one or more miss, and want to have pups from them. Or certain bitches fail to come into heat, and the breeder wants to bring them in. This may be done with hormones, but it is a veterinary matter. The combination of drugs which has produced best results in bringing a bitch into heat is stilbestrol. It may be given in pill form, or right in the food, or it may be injected. After about five days' treatment with five milligrams a day, a 25 lb. bitch will be in heat. After she comes in heat, two milligrams a day will continue the heat normally, but she probably will not ovulate. To produce ovulation we inject her with about 20 units of pregnant mare serum and breed her the next day. Our percentage of fertile matings has been high.

VI
Reproduction in the Male

In the preceding chapter we discussed the part the female plays in reproduction, and mentioned the sperm from the male. These very minute bodies are actually shaped like polliwogs. They are oval and flattish, each having a tail about nine times as long as the body. Each sperm, as we have seen, has half the normal complement of chromosomes.

Sperm, short for *spermatozoa*, are manufactured by the germ plasm of the dog, and this basic mass of cells is part of the *testicles*. The testicles are, in many ways, interesting organs.

They develop within the puppy's body but move outward through slits in the abdominal wall, and are already out of the body and just forward of the sac which holds them later, the *scrotum*, at the time of birth. Sometimes people who should know better compare the descent of the puppy testicles with those of boys', whose testicles do not descend until puberty, but there is no real basis for comparison.

While we are on this subject, we should know the terms which are used for the conditions in which the testicles fail to descend at all. When they

White Miniature, Ch. Lorac's Magic Gay Blade, Mrs. Carol Josephson, Miami Beach, Florida, owner.

Silver Toy, Shadow Box Silver Silhouette, Barbara Ann Woods, Oak Lawn, Illinois, owner.

remain in the abdomen, or when they have come through the abdominal rings but have not progressed far enough to occupy the scrotum, the condition is called *cryptorchidism*.

A *monorchid* is a dog which has only one testicle, or a dog in which only one testicle has grown into the scrotum.

An *anorchid* is a dog without testicles, or one in which the testicles have not grown into the scrotum.

The word grown here may puzzle some readers who have the idea that testicles simply slide down a passageway into a sac. Not at all. The process is one of growth. The testicle, while inside the abdomen, becomes adhered to the tissue lining the abdomen—the *peritoneum*. This then grows downwards through the abdominal slits (rings), and drags the testicle with it. This growth is under the influence of a hormone made by the anterior pituitary gland. It is now manufactured synthetically, and sold under such terms as A.P.L. (Anterior Pituitary Like). If this is injected early in the growth period into a cryptorchid puppy, it often stimulates the descent and renders him normal. In some older pups, when the testicle was close to the scrotum, it has also brought about the desired result. But dogs which have to be treated thus can still pass on the condition to their pups, and are bad risks as breeders. Cryptorchidism is rare in some breeds, and common in others.

Black Standard, Bridget of Belle Glen, Isabelle McMullen, Saddle River, New Jersey, owner.

When testosterone was first offered veterinarians, it was used repeatedly in an effort to correct cryptorchidism, and several reports of success appeared. Later reports indicate that its use is substitutive therapy, and that it is not only useless, but tends to degenerate the testicles.

Sperm are of two kinds: male-forming and female-forming. This capacity is due to the number of chromosomes the sperms possess. Bitches have only one kind of chromosomes, but in a male dogs a pair of them differ. One is called the X and the other the Y. And this is the explanation of sex, for when a male with a Y chromosome combines with an egg possessing a Y, the product is a bitch pup. When the X chromosome combines with a Y chromosome, the pup will be a male.

So theoretically there should be an equal number of dog and bitch pups born, but there are not. There are many more males than females. Those interested in following this study further can consult the book *How to Breed Dogs*. Conceptions occurring in the cold months result in a much higher ratio of males to females. There are influences at work, which we do not as yet understand, modifying the expectancy. But today we have no way of producing sex to order.

The males' testicles are outside the body because the heat inside would prevent the production of sperm. A muscle pulls them close to the body to keep them warm in cold weather and lengthens to permit movement of air and some sweating from the scrotum in hot weather.

The penis of members of the dog family is unique in that, besides being capable of becoming enlarged with blood, it has an area which enlarges much more than the forepart does. When there is no enlargement of the penis, it is quite small. The dog's penis contains a pointed bone which may be felt in the front part, just behind this bone is located the section capable of great enlargement. When the dog copulates with a bitch, the penis is thrust into the vagina, where it instantly swells. The huge enlargement of the bulbous part takes place due to its filling with blood, and it becomes at least three times as large as the rest of the penis. In this way, the dog is tied to the bitch; it is entirely due to the male, the bitch having no part in the initial tieing.

When tieing has occurred, the semen is pumped by spurts into the vagina. Probably then the bitch helps keep the penis enlarged, because there begins a series of peristaltic waves, which causes a slight tightening and relaxing of the vagina. Some males will remain tied (or hung) for five minutes, some for 60. A five-minute tie is just as satisfactory as a longer one, because the semen has been moved up through the uterus and Fallopian tubes to the ovarian capsules by the end of five minutes.

Black Standard, Ch. Estid Ingenue of Syerncrest, Dr. & Mrs. Joseph P. Murphy, Los Angeles, California, owners.

Gigi, full of mischief and in a Dutch clip. Owned by Dr. & Mrs. Herbert Axelrod.

How often may a vigorous stud be bred without harm? Probably once a day will not hurt him. The week before he died, at thirteen years of age, Red Brucie bred seven bitches, all of which conceived. Nature is most generous with sperm. In one good mating a dog may discharge millions of sperm, though a smaller amount is produced by dogs frequently mated. Rams offer an excellent example of the possibilities, for a single ram has been known to impregnate sixty ewes within 24 hours. I have seen a vigorous stud, left with a bitch, copulate five times with her, and remain tied at least 18 minutes each time. The dog showed no signs of weakness. It probably harms the dog not at all, but more than one breeding a day would produce questionable results in the ensuing litters. Some stud-dog owners refuse to permit their dogs to be bred more often than once a week, surely on sentimental, not on scientific grounds.

VII
Rearing Puppies

At the end of her gestation period the expectant mother dog lets you know that she will soon deliver her puppies. You can tell by such behavior as this: She seeks a nest. It may be a hole she digs in the ground, or her kennel bedding may be scratched up and rearranged. If she is a house dog, she may push your shoes together in a corner. If she is loose, you may find her in a secluded corner of your garden. She plainly shows that she wants to be by herself. If you wait for her to have her puppies and then move her to a place of your liking, she may turn against her pups. Even the best mothers become poor ones when disturbed during the first week after whelping.

Just before she whelps, a long haired bitch's hair can be clipped from her breasts to good advantage. If she has been allowed to lie in a run infested with worm eggs, she may have thousands of them stuck to her nipples and to the waxy secretions on the skin. If she is thoroughly cleaned a day or two before she whelps, it may prevent early infestations of her pups by intestinal parasites, and thus remove an obstacle to raising the litter.

Silver Miniature, Ch. Hollycourt Talent of Silver, Miss M. Ruelle Kelchner, Hollycourt Kennels, Millerton, New York, owner.

Most bitches are good mothers. It is seldom necessary to help them, but when you see a bitch straining and accomplishing nothing for several hours, a call to your veterinarian is in order. The average bitch will require about three hours to complete her whelping, but if she has a pup every 90 minutes, or takes six or eight hours to complete the task, it is not necessarily abnormal. Even 24 hours labor can be considered normal in the case of slow whelpers. A tiny amount (1/10 cc.) of Pitocin injected under her skin will hurry a slow whelper remarkably.

If she fails to chew off a sac in which a puppy is born, you must rupture it and slip it off the pup, folding it back over the umbilical cord so she can consume it along with the placenta. She will do as well if you cut the cord off an inch from the puppy and dispose of the placenta as if she were permitted to be natural and eat it. There is doubt that she obtains anything of value from it. Very likely it is a holdover from the days when bitches were their own janitors and kept the nests clean in this way, just as they do when they consume the urine and feces of their puppies.

In this matter of elimination by puppies, it is not generally understood that they tend to hold their urine and feces until the lapping of the mother's tongue causes a relaxation of the sphincters. Persons rearing orphan puppies can keep their boxes perfectly clean by simply wiping the pups with a moist piece of cotton until they eliminate.

Black Miniature, Barkhaven's Matara, Sondern Kennels, Brooklyn, New York, owners.

Black Toy, Ch. Douai Atlanta, Douai Kennels, Haverford, Pennsylvania, owner.

DEWCLAWS

The extra digits on the feet, equivalent to the human thumbs, are called dewclaws. Breeds used for retrieving in water find them useful, but in pets and those used only for upland bird hunting they are often a source of trouble. This is due principally to the fact that the nails on the rear dewclaws do not reach the ground to wear off, and so may grow in a circle and penetrate the toe.

Only a small percentage of dogs possess them anyway, and they are inherited, so may easily be bred out of a strain. If your pups are born with dewclaws which you feel will never be useful to the grown dog, trim them or have them trimmed off early.

Occasionally a bitch will lap a puppy's surgical site and keep it bleeding until she may weaken it greatly. Remember that there is almost a complete absence of iron and some other minerals in bitches' milk, a puppy being born with all he will have until he begins to eat solid food. If he hemorrhages early in life, his precious iron and sodium won't stretch out enough to enable him to live, and he will either be unthrifty or die.

The first food other than milk which puppies receive, if their mothers behave normally, will be partially digested stomach contents. The wild bitch kills rodents or obtains other food, comes home with it, digesting it as she comes, and then vomits among her litter of pups. They wallow in it, eating all they can. When they are done, she eats the remainder and laps them clean.

So, if your bitch acts doglike and unhumanly, don't imagine that she is sick, but accept her actions as natural. You'd be amazed to know how many experienced breeders have brought bitches that behaved in this manner to veterinarians, because they thought the dogs were sick.

WORMING

In Chapter X you will learn about parasites. But here a warning: Puppies can be and often are born infested. The embryonic worms remain dormant until birth, when they start to grow, and by three weeks of age the pups may be anemic from loss of blood to hookworms, or so poisoned from roundworm toxins, that they succumb.

There is no harm done to three-week-old puppies by deworming them if it is done properly. I deworm all of mine then, and again eleven or twelve days later, and have reduced puppy mortality a great deal in this way. In Chapter X the safe doses are given. But if your pup is anemic and weak from worms, no dose is entirely safe. Don't blame the drug or the method then, but blame yourself for permitting the ravages of worms to weaken your pups. If you find the pups prostrate after deworming give them heat and it may revive them. Starvation is extremely necessary, because tetrachlorethylene is soluble in fat, and since bitches' milk is half fat, unless rigid starvation has preceded the drug, you can kill pups with it. But no method I know is so efficient or harmless when properly used.

Black Standard, Bel Tor Flight of Fancy, Mrs. George Lemon, Jr., Ruxton, Maryland, owner.

A Cream White Poodle, Wins Custard of Swan Hill.

WEANING

Weaning is a crucial time in all puppies' lives, and it is a good time to commence weighing your pups to determine whether their growth is satisfactory. By all means start to wean them, and at the same time start to spare their mother, as soon as you can get your pups to eat. By using the right foods, this can be as early as 15 or 16 days.

Experience has shown that puppies do best on rich milk, to which foods containing good-quality protein and some minerals are added. If no Jersey milk is available, add some coffee cream to evaporated milk. And whatever you do, try to modify cows' milk toward bitches' milk, and not toward human milk. Almost all of the older books gave us formulae for simulated human milk, whereas bitches' milk is the very reverse. This table shows the difference:

Black Miniature, Tansy, C. D., Miss Dereke J. Harvey, Hauxhurst Kennels, New York, New York, owner.

The Difference in Composition in Bitch, Cow and Human Milk

	Bitch	Cow	Human
Water	77.0	86.3	87.3
Protein	7.3	3.5	1.3
Sugar	3.7	4.7	7.5
Fat	11.0	4.0	3.5

Instead of adding dextrose (glucose) and lime water, we must add more fat and more proteins, and subtract sugar. Dextrose is sugar, as is lactose, which is milk sugar. Puppies have been raised on such improper diets, but not nearly so well as on one such as this:

Lactogen ....2 oz. by volume
Heavy Cream (30 per cent butter fat)...............2 oz. by volume
Water ....4 oz. by volume

If you make such a mixture, the sugar in the lactogen will be a little higher than the ideal, but I have raised hundreds of pups on it, and so have others. Now don't spoil it, when the pups are old enough to eat solid food, by adding baby cereals to it. Remember that babies require seventeen years to grow, whereas puppies have explosive growth, your pup will be grown in seven months. There are excellent puppy meals to be had, designed for rapid puppy growth and containing all the necessary minerals and vitamins, besides the complete proteins and fats which the explosive growth of puppies requires. For those selling puppies, such a good puppy food is a Godsend, because a small supply may be given or sold with each puppy, which foresight upon your part prevents digestive upsets. You will find that many buyers return puppies to you because of loose stools, which are due only to change of diet. It is well to have the buyer continue on the food your puppies have been eating. If that can be arranged, one source of worry will have been banished.

Some puppy sellers give with each puppy a stupid yet elaborate set of feeding instructions embodying the feeding of a great variety of foods, and causing a lot of trouble in preparation. These lists are entirely unnecessary, and simply show the buyer that you are a generation behind the times in your knowledge of dog feeding. Science has demonstrated that all this fuss is absurd, and that a high-grade meal food, plus fat and milk for the young pup, will do a better job, and that variety is not necessary.

HERNIA

As the puppy grows, you may note a small lump over the umbilicus or navel. A high percentage of pups fail to heal across completely, and the bulge you feel is a hernia. In such a slight deformity there is no danger unless the opening through the abdomen is sufficiently large to permit a loop of intestine to work out into the sac you feel. If it is small, the sac will eventually harden into a lump which never harms the dog and is not noticeable. If the orifice is large enough to allow the intestine to work through, have your veterinarian repair it before a strangulation occurs.

Black Toy, Ch. Kenbrook Forest Bodka, Dr. Ralph A. Logan & Edward B. Jenner, Libertyville, Illinois, owners.

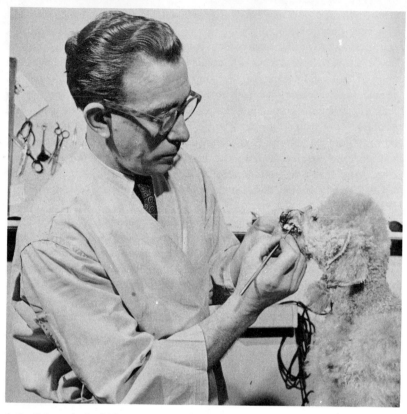

A Poodle's teeth should be kept clean of tartar. Permitting your Poodle to chew hard dog biscuits regularly is one way to keep the teeth clean. Another is to have the tartar scraped.

TEETH

At very close to fourteen weeks of age the two upper middle incisors will loosen and be pushed out by a new pair. Then the teeth will gradually all fall out and be replaced. If, at this crucial time, the puppy has any sickness which disturbs his metabolism, the enamel will not be deposited on the teeth. If they are partway in, you will eventually find a ring around the teeth. If the sickness occurred earlier, only the tips of the teeth may be pitted and discolored. It used to be thought that only "distemper" caused such disfigurement, but today we know better; many ailments can cause it.

In Chapter IX we shall consider vaccinations against various diseases, so we need not go into the problem here.

The kennel clubs insist upon litter registrations before the individual puppies of the litter may be registered. Since this process requires several weeks, it is well to send in the application, properly filled out, and have the

Sporting a Dutch clip and a sequin studded collar, no wonder he looks proud.

litter registration in your hands by the time the puppies are old enough to sell. You can thus be ready to give each buyer a completed individual registration application with the litter. This foresight, too, saves headaches.

It is highly important to sell your pups at as early an age as possible, because you will get no more for them once they are out of the cute puppy stage than you will when they are seven weeks old, and often less. So advertising should be planned well in advance to appear at the proper time. Newspaper ads seldom bring the buyers willing to pay what those who read the national magazines will pay. In the former case you will answer many phone calls from those wanting $5.00 pups; in the latter, there will be voluminous correspondence from those who want to know the ancestry back to Adam.

Have some photos of the parents and litter if possible. This will save hours of writing.

VIII
Your Dog's Food

I could tell you in one short paragraph how to feed a dog or a whole kennel full, but dog owners want to know why, hence a whole chapter.

There are as many ways to feed dogs as there are dogs. There is no one best way, since local conditions vary greatly, and certain foods are available to some and not to others. In my book *Feeding our Dogs* I have a long list of widely differing, but successful, methods of dog feeding. And the differences are amazing in their scope.

We are told that the natural food of cats and dogs consists of rodents, such as mice or rabbits. But wouldn't a cat owner look suspicious if he spent part of a day trapping mice to feed his cat! Wolves, the probable ancestors of dogs, besides eating rodents, killed larger species and ate the stomach and intestinal contents as well as the muscular meat. But who is going to the slaughter-house to buy stomach contents for his dog and add them to muscular meat? Once I did feed about five tons of this in research, but I didn't smell like

Dogs like to eat from the same type of dish at every meal and it's a good idea to place the dishes in the same spot at each meal. When the meal is over, leave only the water available.

Putting a raincoat on the dog when he must go out in the rain makes housekeeping easier, and less combing necessary.

honeysuckle each time the mixing was over. Yes, the dogs like it. My wife didn't. The idea was impractical.

So you and I, being sensible, realize we can't offer our dogs their natural food, so we try to approximate it and fulfill all their nutritional requirements. How can we best do it?

Protein. This important dietary essential may be supplied by feeding meat, fish, milk, cheese, or vegetable matter of high-protein content, such as soy bean meal. We can use these ingredients fresh, frozen, or dried. If they are dried, they will be better preserved by the vacuum process, which dries at temperatures well below the boiling point, thus removing only water and doing almost no harm to proteins or vitamins.

Miniature, Ch. Fontclair Festoon, Dunwalke Kennels, Far Hills, New Jersey, owner.

Silver Toy, Miniken's Slipper Silverman, Mr. & Mrs. Turbin, owners.

Carbohydrates. If we take bitches' milk as a guide to an ideal ration, we find it is composed of about 29 per cent protein, 13 per cent carbohydrate, and 43 per cent fat. If we take a whole woodchuck as another guide, we find the carbohydrate considerably higher because of the stomach contents, and the fat about 30 per cent. Research has shown that a diet with 50 per cent carbohydrate is satisfactory (on a dry basis, of course).

Carbohydrates may be supplied as starches and sugars. Some dog biscuits contain 85 per cent baked starch. Baking turns starch into dextrin, which tastes sweet, and dogs like it. Syrups are fed in fairly large quantities to dogs in the form of sweetening in corn flakes. There is plenty of starch-digesting enzyme, to handle even more starch, in the fluids discharged into dogs' intestines; but when too much is fed, the protein percentage naturally goes down as the carbohydrate rises.

Fat. If more than 25 per cent (on a dry basis) of a sedentary dog's diet is fat, his excretions will be too soft. A hunting dog can handle 40 per cent fat while he is exercising hard.

Fat may be fed as suet, lard, lamb, fish, chicken, and bacon fats, or even vegetable shortening. The dog uses it, deposits the unnecessary unused part in his tissues as adipose and, in time, turns this fat into dog fat. From each unit of fat he gets two and one quarter times as much energy as he does when his body burns protein and carbohydrate. So the use of fat is one way to save money feeding dogs. At 1960 prices, fat costs about 5 cents a pound at any butcher's. If dry dog food costs 12 cents a pound, then fat is actually worth 30 cents. Too bad we can't feed over 25 per cent in the ration!

Fat has valuable nutritional qualities. The fat-soluble vitamins are stored in body fat. Sometimes beef suet is actually yellow from Vitamin A. Puppies, but not grown dogs require Vitamin E, and if a lactating bitch is fed plenty of fat, the puppies will get it in this way as well as from grains.

Then, too, fat insures better digestion of other foods because in some way it causes the dog's food to pass more slowly through his intestines. It also spares vitamins of the B-complex, possibly because of greater bacterial activity within the dog's intestines.

And fat, because it is so easily assimilated, produces a plump appearance in dogs and growing puppies.

Toy, Ch. Buttonwood Ballet, Manuel Miyares, Malmyr Kennels, Metairie, Louisiana, owner.

Miniature, Ch. Cappoquin Bon Fiston, Cappoquin Kennels, New Hope, Pennsylvania, owner.

Calories. While they are not an ingredient of food, we must take heat units represented by calories into consideration, in order to know how much food a dog requires. These hardy little fellows will almost all eat at least 30 per cent more than they need for daily requirements, and some 50 per cent. A well-fed dog is always hungry enough to snatch and eat avidly a crust of bread from one's hand. Because they are such "easy keepers" as the stockman says, one must always be watching them for their tendency to become overweight. Some people call them gluttons, really a highly complimentary term, because it must be realized that no normal dog ever needs pampering to get it to eat. A dog that is not hungry is either sick or "spoiled rotten."

Here are the amounts I have found mature dogs of various weights require to maintain weight under kennel conditions:

TABLE 1

Pounds of Dog	Calorie Requirement	Canned Food	Dry Food	Beef Muscle	Eggs (average size)	Fat	Dog Biscuits
5	250	½ can	3½ ozs.	3¾ ozs.	2	¾ ozs.	2 ozs.
10	500	1 ,,	5½ ,,	7 ,,	3-4	1¼ ,,	4 ,,
15	625	1¼ ,,	7 ,,	10 ,,	5	2 ,,	6 ,,
20	760	1⅔ ,,	8½ ,,	13 ,,	6-7	2½ ,,	8½ ,,
25	1000	2 ,,	11 ,,	16½ ,,	7-8	3 ,,	10 ,,
30	1175	2⅓ ,,	13½ ,,	20 ,,	8-9	3¾ ,,	10½ ,,
40	1450	3⅓ ,,	1 lb.	25 ,,	12	4¾ ,,	12½ ,,
50	1750	4 ,,	1¼ ,,	31 ,,	14	6¾ ,,	15½ ,,
60	2000	4½ ,,	1½ ,,	36 ,,	16	7½ ,,	18 ,,

Of course one can't feed all meat and expect his dogs to remain in condition, and obviously one can't feed an all-fat diet. The table shows the relative values of foods. "Dog biscuits" include crushed biscuits (kibble). It is clear that the best buy is fat, but we shall discuss this matter later.

Silver Toy, Ch. Ro-Mary's Silver Rhythm, Mr. & Mrs. Ralph Bosso, Whiffletree Kennels, Bernardsville, New Jersey, owners.

Minerals. Everyone has heard and read of the importance of the various minerals to us and to our dogs. If one is feeding a good prepared ration, this aspect of diet can be forgotten; if one is feeding his dogs what he eats himself, it can also be forgotten if the owner himself is healthy. But if one is feeding one's dog only what the dog likes most, the question of minerals becomes exceedingly important. If one is feeding that old mixture of kibbles, meat, cod-liver oil, and vegetables, again minerals must also be added.

TABLE 2

Cost of maintaining a 25 pound dog per day and for one year on the following feeding methods (900 calories a day).

Method	Cost per day	Cost per year
1. Table Scraps	$.50	$182.5
2. Canned dog food (2 for 29¢)	.29	105.85
3. Kibbles, Meat, Vegetables (18¢, 50¢, & 5¢ per pound) Supplements (5¢ per day)	.38	138.70
4. Pellets (15¢ per lb.)	.084	30.66
5. Dry Egg	.078	28.47
6. Dry Dog Food plus Fat (14¢ per lb.; fat, free)	.04	15.70

Table 3 shows the minerals and their principal sources and abundance in foods usually fed dogs. This is for those who want to mix their own foods. By *mixing* I mean putting together various foods such as milk, eggs, meat, vegetables, vitamin concentrates, minerals, and so forth. *Mixing* can also be taken to mean mixing dry food.

Vitamins. If you use a good dry food, you can also just forget all about the word vitamins. These dietary essentials are so cheap that no food manufacturer who cares about his reputation leaves any out of his food mixtures. But if you mix your own rations, it may pay you to add a drop, no more, of percomorph oil for each dog daily, to provide vitamins A and D, and a spoonful of brewers' yeast for the B-complex vitamins. Your meats will supply B1 and B2. If you want to be sure your dogs have enough of the essential fatty acids linoleic, linolenic, and arachidonic, give each dog two drops of raw linseed oil a day.

Table 4 lists the principal vitamins and their sources.

TABLE 3
MINERALS: THEIR FUNCTIONS AND SOURCES

	FUNCTIONS IN BODY	PRINCIPAL SOURCES
Calcium 90% of body calcium is in the bones; 1% in circulation Stored in body	Bone building, rickets preventive Blood component Reproduction Lactation Muscle function Nerve function Heart function Tooth component	Bones and bone meal Alfalfa-leaf meal Milk
Phosphorus Bones, blood, muscles and teeth	Bone building Tooth component Carbohydrate metabolism Fat metabolism Blood component Ricket preventive Liquid content of tissues	Cereals Meat Fish Bones Milk So abundant in dog diets it is of little concern to owners

Silver Standard, Douai Gay Ghost of Meritor, Mrs. Richard A. Coffman & Douai Kennels, Haverford, Pennsylvania, owners.

Standard, Ch. Carillon Dilemma, Miss Blanche Saunders, Carillon Kennels, Bedford, New York, owner.

Miniature, Rothars Merrymorn Nell Rose, Mass Oaks Kennels, New Orleans, La., owner.

Iron

Composes only 4/1000ths of the body weight	Component of red blood cells	Egg yolk
		Liver
	Transports oxygen in blood	Kidney
Needed in minute quantities		Gizzard
	65% is found in blood	Heart
Is stored in body	30% is found in liver, bone marrow and spleen	Bone marrow
		Meats
	5% is found in muscle tissue	

Potassium

	Body fluid regulator	Blood
	Helps regulate blood	Potatoes
	Muscular function	Vegetables

Sodium

Found in body in combination with phosphorus, chlorine, and sulphur	Regulates body fluids	Table Salt
	Blood regulator	Blood
	Component of gastric juice	
	Component of urine	

Miniature, Beaufresne White King, Mrs. Gardner Cassatt, Villanova, Penna., owner

Chlorine

Found combined with sodium and hydrogen	Component of gastric juice	Table salt
	Blood regulator	Blood
	Regulates body fluids	
	Component of urine	

Iodine

Most of iodine in body is found in thyroid gland	Thyroid health and normal growth	Foods grown in iodine-rich soils
	Regulates metabolism	Iodized salt
	Prevents goiter and cretinism	Fish meal made from salt-water fish
	In formation of thyroxine	Shellfish

Silver Miniature, Perrevan Coupon, Elizabeth Van Sciver, Malvern, Penna., owner.

Magnesium

Needed only in minute amounts

Muscle activity
Bone building
Normal growth
Nerve function
Blood function

Bones
Vegetables
Epsom salts

Copper

Needed only in minute amounts

Forms hemoglobin with iron

Blood
Copper Sulfate

Sulphur

Minute amounts required but needed regularly

Body regulation
Combination in salts as sulfates

Meat
Egg yolk
Any food which, when decomposed, smells like bad eggs

TABLE 4
VITAMINS: THEIR PROPERTIES, FUNCTIONS AND SOURCES

VITAMINS	CONCERNED WITH	COMMON SOURCES
A (and carotene)	General living	Alfalfa-leaf meal
Stable at boiling temperatures	Growth	Butter
	Skin health	Carrots
Spoils with age if exposed to air	Muscle co-ordination	Egg yolks
	Fertility	Fish livers
Body stores it	Digestion	Glandular organs
Fat soluble	Hearing	Leaves of plants
	Vision	Milk, whole
	Prevention of infection	Spinach
	Nerve health	Many dark green vegetables
	Pituitary-gland function	Fish-liver oils
		Synthetic vitamin A
		Carotine
B Complex		
Biotin	Growth promotion	Yeast
Pantothenic acid	Nerve health	Cereals
Riboflavin, thiamin	Heart health	Milk
Folic acid	Liver function	Eggs
Niacin	Appetite	Liver
Pyridoxin	Gastro-intestinal function	Alfalfa-leaf meal
Animal protein factor		Rapidly growing plants
Water soluble	Intestinal absorption	Bacterial growth
Body-storage small	Lactation	Cattle paunch and intestinal contents
Some destroyed by high cooking temperatures, but not riboflavin	Fertility	
	Muscle function	
	Prevention of anemia	
Biotin effects robbed by raw egg white	Prevention of black tongue	
	Prevention of Vincent's disease	
	Kidney and bladder function	
	Blood health	

VITAMINS	CONCERNED WITH	COMMON SOURCES
D		
Irradiated ergosterol	Regulation of calcium and phosphorus in blood	Fish livers and oils extracted
Well stored by body		Some animal fats
Stands considerable heat	Calcium and phosphorus metabolism	
Resists decomposition	Prevention of rickets	
Fat soluble	Normal skeletal development	
	Muscular co-ordination	
	Lactation	
E		
Tocopherol	Survival of young puppies	Seed germs
Fat soluble		Germ oils
Body stores it		
Perishes when exposed to air		
Stands ordinary cooking temperatures		
K		
Fat soluble	Blood-clotting	Alfalfa-leaf meal
	Young puppy health	
Unsaturated Fatty Acids (sometimes called vitamin F)		
Linoleic acid	Coat and skin health	Wheat-germ oil
Linolenic acid		Linseed oil
Arachadinic acid		Rapeseed oil
		Many seed oils

Apricot Toy, Ch. Meisen Bit O'Gold, Hilda Meisengahl, Meisen Poodles, North Hollywood, California, owner.

COMMON FEEDING METHODS

Table 2 shows graphically about how much it costs, per day and per year, to maintain a mature 25 pound dog. And it costs just about two and one third times as much to raise a puppy by these methods from weaning to eight months as it does to maintain a mature dog. The six pound puppy consumes as much as a 15 pound mature dog but the 24 pound pup eats as much as a 60 pound mature dog and then at maturity, his appetite suddenly dwindles.

Now we shall discuss the methods:

1. **Table scraps.** In this day of refrigeration, in almost every home there is no such things as table scraps, unless the housewife is wasteful. All food for human beings can be kept until it is eaten. If it is spoiled for human consumption it should not be fed to dogs. Garbage today should be only bones, fruit peelings, and the like. Once any housewife starts feeding table scraps to a dog, she starts buying extra food, without even admitting to herself that some is for the dog. It then costs one fourth as much to feed a mature dog as it does to feed a member of the family; and this is an absurd extravagance. Practically the only real table scrap to save for the dog is the surplus grease you would otherwise throw away. And this, if wisely used, makes your dog cost less to feed, not more.

If you insist on feeding table scraps you might as well go all out for it and treat the dog as another member of the family. If you neglect to make the family order big enough so the dog has something, then give him canned dog food to fill in and a few dog biscuits.

There are lots of old wives' tales about what not to feed a dog. No starch (therefore no potato), no fat, no sugar, or he'll get worms, no milk or he'll get more worms. All nonsense! A dog can digest any of these things as well as we can. If you feed him milk or candy, it is true that he gets finicky and won't eat his regular meal as he should. If he gets potatoes in lumps, he generally passes them as lumps in his evacuations, because dogs seldom chew easily swallowed food. So if you feed potatoes, mash them first.

How can sweets or milk "make worms"? I often ask clients, who tell me that they do, whether they ever eat sweets or drink milk. The way dogs get worms is from ingesting worm eggs, by swallowing fleas, or by eating infected rabbits from which they contract the tapeworms. It's to be hoped no worm eggs get into our milk containers or on our candy.

Toy, Jalen's Percette, Allen C. Warder & Jane Speiser, Jalen Kennels, Fort Lauderdale, Florida, owners.

Miniature, Ch. Bric A Brac Brand New, Seafren Kennels, Mechanicsville, Penna., owner.

2. **Canned Dog Food.** This is food for those who don't care how much it costs to feed their dogs. Look on the labels, and you will see that almost all canned foods contain from 70 per cent to 74 per cent water. So about a quarter of the can is food; the rest you can get free from your faucet. Now if four ounces of food is worth 17 cents to you—which makes it 68 cents a pound, the price of excellent meat, buy it. There are many fine foods in cans on the market, but don't let any manufacturer convince you that your dog can live on half a can a day, as some labels state. If fed canned food exclusively, any lively 25 pound dog needs two cans a day, and will eat more.

There are also some pretty awful canned foods, too. These are the ones you seldom see advertised. One company uses half-a-dozen different labels for the same food. If you happen to be a person who judges a food's value by how greedily your dog eats it, and if you are inclined to overfeed, then you may try one label and because the dog isn't hungry enough to eat the food, he refuses it and you say it's no good. By afternoon his appetite has improved. You try the same food with a different label and he eats it. "Wonderful food! That's the food for my dog from now on." Don't be deceived.

There are some good ones, too, which are not advertised but are sold cheaply, the makers hoping the low price will move the food. All companies that make good foods have experimental kennels, and are certain the diet is right before it is offered to the public.

3. **Kibbles, Meat, and Vegetables.** And of course cod-liver oil. Thousands of dogs have been raised and maintained on this mixture usually with liberal amounts of other vitamin and mineral concentrates added. Some kibbled biscuits are vastly better than others. On some the animals on test die in a few months. Kibbles are today a complete diet. They have great taste appeal. The starch-flour being the chief ingredient, having been converted largely to dextrin by baking, tastes sweet and the dogs generally find it to their liking. Add ground or canned meat and boiled green vegetables and you have a fairly good food.

This diet is troublesome to mix. It is a nuisance to buy and refrigerate meat or to open cans, and obtaining and cooking vegetables are laborious. And when you have added the tonics, have you done any better for your dogs than you would have done by feeding them some other way? Let's see.

Silver Miniature, Ch. Round Table's Avocat, Round Table Kennels, Middletown, Del., owner.

4. **Pellets.** A number of commercial foods are now available in pellet form. Some are large pellets, an inch long and of various diameters. Some are only an eighth of an inch thick and not much longer. These may go by the name of *meal*, which is claimed to be homogenized. It is not, but the pelleting keeps the meal from sifting into layers, and it looks attractive to the housewife and pours easily. The makers suggest either dry feeding or else the addition of only a small amount of water, the dogs having to drink the balance to supply enough for digestion of the food. The pellets may be left in one pan and water in another, but in the case of small pellets the water pan soon becomes offensively dirty, and must be changed quite frequently.

5. **Meal Type.** This is often referred to in the trade as dry dog food. Since pellets are made from the same general formula, it might seem sensible to consider them with the meal types, but I do not because the latter are so much more versatile. Pellets have not found acceptance in kennel practice, while meals have. There are considerable differences among the many meals now on the market. Some have 30 per cent more protein than others, and some double the amount of fat which others carry. The minerals are some-

Standard, Tally-Ho Top Secret, Mrs. Leonard Bonney, Oyster Bay, New York, owner.

Standard, Ch. Puttencove Promise, Puttencove Kennels, Manchester, Mass., owner.

times so high as to be above the maximum for certain state laws. One of the most popular foods was thus outlawed from one of our states because it had 11 per cent calcium and phosphorus. And I know dog owners feeding it who were adding tri-calcium phosphate as well! Ground bone is the cheapest ingredient added to dog foods, so one need never add any more of the chemicals of which bone is composed, namely, calcium and phosphorus.

Today almost all of the meals available have been industriously studied by nutritional scientists, and have been constantly improved. If there is any one kind of food which tends to be better than the others, it is meal. Moreover, one can add fat to it and make an economical ration.

Mix $1\frac{1}{2}$ ounces of fat with 5 ounces of a high-quality meal, and you have 850 calories of the best food you can find. You couldn't beat it if you spent $100 a day.

This mixture will contain every known dietary essential. If you add any supplements, you are not only throwing away your money, but upsetting a formula which probably cost thousands of dollars to compound and test.

A Silver Poodle in a Dutch Clip.

Miniature, Ch. Beaujeu Regal, Bobby L. Crutchfield, Austin, Texas, owner.

Any number of fine, healthy dogs thrived on this diet. It supports reproduction wonderfully well; it reduces whelping troubles; pups are not born with cleft palates and harelips nearly so often as they are from dams raised on other diets. Such defects were almost unheard of in my dogs.

This diet also supports growth. Some dogs will be full grown in seven months. I've had some breeds full grown in 27 weeks. But they will eat food worth about 10 cents a day as they near maturity, and then when they reach it the food consumption drops enough to be alarming, if you are unprepared for it.

Meals and fat will support lactation (milk production) quite well, but more protein will be necessary for extra-large litters. This can be added as dried skim milk, dried whale meat, coddled eggs if you can buy them cheaply from a hatchery and cook them, or beef or horse meat. No more than 25 per cent to 30 per cent of these ingredients will be needed for large litters if the dam is a good milker.

EXTRUDED FOODS

As this book goes to press a new kind of food has made its appearance on the market. In an amazingly short time it has become the best selling dog food. Because of this fact many manufacturers are following in the footsteps of the one which pioneered it. The manufacturer of the machinery in which

Toy Black Orchid of Wembley Downs, Mrs. Carruth Maguire, Kansas City, Missouri, owner.

it is made naturally wants to sell his machines and has interested several dog food companies in them.

Extruded food is the name given to those which are made in this manner. The same principle is employed as is used in the manufacture of puffed wheat and rice. The food is heated under great pressure. The pressure is suddenly released in the process and the starch granules explode.

We mentioned that dogs do not digest large raw starch granules such as that found in raw corn meal, and we noted that when the starch is cooked the granules are ruptured and softened so the dog can digest much more of it. The starch is converted into dextrin and becomes sweeter too.

In the extruding process the starch granules are even more fully ruptured, something like the process of popping corn. Here the tight jacket holds the starch until the sudden release of pressure when the jacket bursts and liberates the starch granules. Everyone knows how they expand into many times the original volume.

Extruded foods as sold in 1960 are, in some cases, popped into double the volume of the original and, as they are sold, contain about half the nutritional value of other excellent rations. Thus dogs eat them eagerly because the dogs are almost always hungry, for they obtain only half as much nourishment from the extruded food as they did from a good kibbled or meal-type food they may have formerly eaten.

Kennel owners are not fooled by this new departure; it is the pet dog owner who is. He or she often sits enjoying watching the pet eat and when he smacks his lips and begs for more, this owner naturally concludes, "Now at last I have found *the* food for my pet." Of course he eats and eats because the bulk without nourishment makes him eat eagerly and often if he is to maintain his weight.

Except for the reduction in the number of calories in any given quantity, the essential ingredients are not harmed to any extent by the process. Some of the extruded foods are complete nutritionally; only the dogs have to eat twice as much volume to obtain all the amino acids, fats, minerals and vitamins which they need.

Toy, Ch. Pixdown Little Bit, Pixdown Kennels, Wilton, Connecticut, owner.

WEANING PUPPIES

Remember that your bitch produces light cream, so when you wean the pups you have raised, start them off on rich food. So often dog owners feed them Pablum or Seravim and cows' milk. Some even add lime water and dextrose, as if the little pups were human infants. Make their formula rich in fat and protein, almost the exact opposite of human milk.

Mix some light cream with a regular puppy food such as Pampa, the only one I know of readily available. Then there will be no trouble with the transition from dog milk to your formula.

REDUCING

Every owner learns how gluttonous his pet really is, a mark of great vitality. So overfeeding is always a temptation. When dogs become overweight, due to ignorance, lack of will power on the part of the owner, or neighbors' misplaced generosity, it is hard to refuse the appeal in those melting eyes,

Toy, Douai Overture, Norman Austin, Baliwick Kennels, High Point, North Carolina, owner.

Standard, Ch. Puttencove Brigadier, Mrs. Angela M. Olcott, Swarthmore, Penna., owner.

but do it. Don't let your dog get fat. And urge neighbors also to resist the appeal.

To reduce any dog is a simple matter. Just remember that any animal stores surplus food, in the form of fat, for a rainy day. He can literally live on that fat for months, not days. To reduce him requires exactly the same treatment as we give ourselves when we are overweight: use the accumulated fat for food; don't eat so much; make it a long, rainy day. If a dog needs 900 calories a day, give him a cup of dog meal and the water it takes to moisten it, and absolutely nothing else but water *ad lib*. He will be eating 500 calories, and must consume 400 from the fat on his body. Each pound of fat burns up to 4,000 calories, so he should reduce by about one tenth of a pound a day. That is if some miscreant in your home isn't slipping him tidbits, to defeat your attempt to increase his longevity via weight reduction.

Miniature, Ch. La Foy's Little Commotion, C. D., Mr. & Mrs. J. Kilburn King, New Rochelle, New York, owners.

EXERCISE

Dogs can live to a ripe old age if kept at their proper weight with no more exercise than they get walking about an apartment. You can exercise your dog by long walks, by training him to hunt if you enjoy bird hunting, but the easiest method for you when you are tired by a hard day's work is to spend fifteen minutes throwing a ball for your canine friend to retrieve.

You'll have no trouble teaching the retrieving part. As soon as the dog knows that to drop the ball in your hand means that you will throw it again for him, you can start the exercising process. A mile has 1,760 yards. Suppose you throw the ball 50 yards. He runs and retrieves it, and has run 100 yards. Repeat that eighteen times and your dog has run a mile, while you have remained in one place.

If you want some profitable exercise and live near a golf course, wait until evening, when the golfers have all gone home. Take Ruffles out and throw a golf ball: he will retrieve it. Now make believe to throw it. He will watch the direction you indicate, which will, of course, be out in the rough where golfers lose balls. Ruffles will return with a golf ball in his mouth. A dog belonging to one of my friends retrieved 42 golf balls in one evening. If no one else near you knows this trick, you had better take along a bag to hold the balls your pockets won't contain.

This will also harden Ruffles' muscles and help him reduce, but, unless his diet be restricted, his increased appetite will more than atone for the expenditure of energy.

IX
Diseases

Not according to their importance, but according to their time of appearance, will the diseases of puppies be considered. Nor have we the space to consider them in detail. Books specializing in diseases and treatments can be consulted. The veterinarian is available to you for the specialized help he is prepared to give. Here we consider the important features of the different diseases so that the breeder may recognize the fact that illness is present and needs treatment.

At the outset, let us confess that we know very little about the many diseases of puppies. One of the reasons for this sad state of affairs has been the reluctance of those interested in dogs to think that any disease which causes sniffling and runny noses in puppies could be anything other than distemper. But today, with the real distemper recognized, and the realization that it is becoming less prevalent in some communities, it behooves us all to try to learn what these diseases of puppies really are.

Variety Winners, illustrating the three sizes: Toy, Ch. Fieldstream's Valentine, Mrs. Audrey Kelch, owner. Miniature, Ch. Cappoquin Bon Jongleur, Col. E. E. Ferguson, owner. Standard, Ch. Puttencove Moonshine, Puttencove Kennels, owner.

Toy, Riallen's Verbena Bon Soir, Kathleen T. Partlow, Louisville, Kentucky, owner.

NAVEL INFECTION

When puppies lie on soft beds this trouble practically never occurs, but when they are left on rough boards or on concrete, it is likely to kill every one of a litter. Infection enters through the unhealed navel and spreads rapidly under the skin. There is a moisture and an obnoxious odor about the spot. The bitch cannot lick it clean because her tongue cannot reach as far as the infection has penetrated, and the infection continues to spread in an ever expanding circle. Constant wearing on a rough surface may also penetrate the abdomen until the organs are exposed. The puppy becomes dehydrated and feels stiff to the touch. He may cry more than he should and usually dies in about three days.

Once you observe such a spot in one puppy, you must look over every puppy and see that those surfaces which are worn, even though the infection has not penetrated the skin, are medicated. You should also see that there is plenty of bedding under the puppies in order that no further irritation can occur. Finally, the infected pup or pups must be treated surgically. No halfway measures seem to cure the malady.

The veterinarian will lift the skin and scrape every bit of infected tissue away. He will then apply disinfectant medicine to destroy any bacteria and if

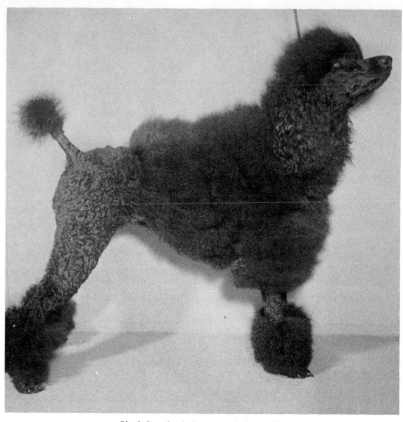

Black Standard almost ready for a clip.

the opening is not too wide, may suture it so that the skin can heal together. It is the lowest layer of skin which has the power of joining with the same on the other side when the two are approximated. If the infection has eaten away this layer, as it often does, there is no point in suturing the dead skin. It is better to trim the skin away up to the point where it is alive and let it grow together from the sides.

Taking care of a puppy with a navel infection sounds easier than it is. You get precious little cooperation from the puppy who seems compelled to lie on this point of his belly. It is essential that the raw spot be well medicated with some healing lotion. If you cannot obtain the services of a veterinarian, try one of the household remedies such as Unguentine, sulfa salves or mild healing powders, etc.

Cover the spot with a bandage. The results of treatment are better in females than in males; because the bandage on males comes so close to the penis that it is constantly wet, and the mother licks it more than she does a bandage on a female. I have had best results from putting adhesive tape around the puppy's body over the bandage. Then each day I cut the tape lengthwise across the belly, change the bandage, and put more tape to hold it in place. This obviates hairs pulling out of the pup's back in removing the tape daily. While the area is healing, the puppy is growing. It may take ten days to heal, by which time the pup is twice as large as he was when treatment was begun. All of the tape around his body will not need to be changed during that time; only that which applied daily over the dressing.

Silver Standard in Dutch Clip & fancy collar.

EYE INFECTIONS

In the very young puppy, sometimes one not over seven days old, a bulge will occasionally be seen under the eyelids, possibly on both eyes. If you make a small opening at the nose end of the slit between the lids with a not-too-sharp instrument, a few drops of pus will run out. This infection has always been due to a *Staphylococcus* type of organism in every affected puppy which I have treated.

Anyone can see that such a swelling is developing. If it is not removed, the pus may damage the eyes, so that it will remain blue and opaque for several weeks, or may destroy the eye completely. Fortunately the eye starts to open at the tenth day and there are not many days in which the pus can do damage. Nevertheless, it should be removed at the very earliest sign.

Several of the mild germ killers which are not harmful to eyes may be used to clear up this infection, but you must be judicious in selection of the proper one because when it is applied, it will be in a pocket with the eyeball. It does not wash out, as ophthalmic medicants do when they irritate. Let your

Some Poodles lie down with legs stretched out behind like a frog, but they generally outgrow this habit as they mature.

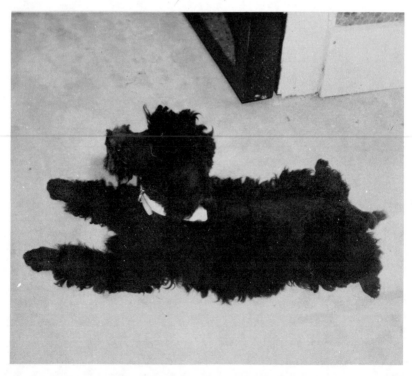

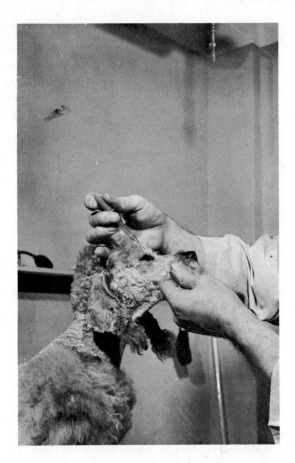

The proper way to instill fluid into a Poodle's eye. Pulling out the lower lid forms a small pocket to hold the liquid.

veterinarian direct the treatment. He may use 5% sulfathaladine or sulfathiazole ophthalmic ointments. Both have proved 100% effective in my experience, as has penicillin.

An eye disorder of puppies, though not an infection, is the inverted third eyelid (nictitating membrane) which causes the protrusion of a gland in the nasal side of the eye, giving the appearance of a little oblong tumor. Sometimes the membrane can be tipped back and the gland tucked in so it will stay. A little zinc sulphate ophthalmic ointment may be sufficiently astringent to shrink it so it will stay. If this measure is unsuccessful, snipping off the gland usually ends the trouble.

Most puppy eye disorders are caused by scratches of other puppies whose sharp little nails are almost like needles. Trim your puppies' nails regularly from the time they are three weeks old. Many otherwise lovely puppies are ruined by eye scratches.

Miniature, Blaujeu Richelieu Ruffles, Mrs. Dore Goldstein, Fort Worth, Texas, owner.

DIARRHEA IN VERY YOUNG PUPPIES

Sometimes as early as the third day, you will hear your little puppies crying pitifully and find them pushed away from their mother who practically disowns them. There is a foul acrid odor about them. The area around the anus, hind legs, and tail is wet. The mother has refused to lick this, and the puppies have become increasingly repulsive to her. They soon are dehydrated, lose their appetites, grow stiff and die, usually emitting pitiful cries almost to the end. Indeed the process is quite pathetic, and you may become frantic wondering what you can do, while watching your puppies dropping away one at a time.

This symptom of diarrhea is probably characteristic of several diseases. So little work has been done on it we know very little about it. It used to be said that acid milk was the cause, but acid milk is normal, as we have seen. One terrific siege in my kennels killed about three-fourths of all the puppies born one spring. Bacteriologists undertook a study, located the responsible bacterium and found it in all the organs and blood. It has never before been described as accomplishing such devastating work.

Another different bacterium caused a similar attack recently and many puppies were lost in three litters. When a fourth came, three puppies began to show the wetness around the tail and gave off the characteristic odor. They died, and might be said to be checks against the next two puppies which showed it. A mixture of sulfathaladine powder and apple pectin has been most successful in my kennels. It is hardly likely that either sulfaguanadine[e] or sulfathaladine will destroy organisms which have left the intestines and are in the blood and organs. It is necessary to have these drugs administered very soon after the trouble starts.

Another remedy which seems to help materially is giving acidophilus milk instead of mother's milk. When I used this method, two feedings of the acidophilus milk put a number of puppies on their feet, but those which were far enough gone to refuse food were not helped even when it was given via a stomach tube.

DIARRHEA IN OLDER PUPPIES

Diarrhea in older puppies can be caused by such a wide variety of things that we must admit a whole book could be written on this subject alone; this is not an exaggeration. Diarrhea is more often than not a result of disease, parasitic infection or laxative diet, but some bacteria which we shall consider can also produce the symptom. Carre distemper, heavy roundworm infestations, and skim milk or improper fiber in the diet are among the chief causes. All but the first are easily corrected.

Toy, Karja's Fairtale In Jet, Mrs. Karl Rudzik, Valley Stream, New York, owner

We should try to eliminate every possible cause before we treat for diarrhea and we often have to learn the cause by the process of elimination. This takes time and puppies are often lost through the best of intentions. I often think, when I hear veterinarians criticized for not having at once hit upon the true cause of a diarrhea, of an experience I had with an outstanding doctor. The patient, a woman had a most unusual ailment and a consultation of eight of the foremost physicians in New York City had been called. Each of their diagnoses was written on a sheet of paper, which my friend gave me to observe while he was making his diagnosis. Every diagnosis was different! Remember that diarrhea has a multitude of causes, and don't condemn your veterinarian because he can't say within five minutes of seeing your puppy exactly what the trouble is. The competent doctor will explore all possibilities before starting treatment.

Bacteria of various types have been implicated in the diarrhea of puppies between one week and eight weeks of age. This is sometimes curable, and sometimes not. Whole litters are often wiped out when the wrong organism obtains a foothold.

In seven litters which came to my attention within one month, cultures of the stools showed large numbers of a *Salmonella*, a bacterium which produces hydrogen sulphide. This substance causes fits, pains, prostration, loss of appetite and together with the toxins elaborated by the organism, death.

Miniature, Ch. Highland Sand George, Mrs. James Farrell, Tiro, Ohio, owner.

Miniature Puppy, Woodland's Snow Flake, Mrs. Douglas R. Adams, South Plainfield, New Jersey, owner.

However, the period of sickness in the puppies is quite prolonged. The little fellows start lying around in their pens crying pitifully and day by day become weaker until they die. You may hope to see at least two or three recover, but it is generally expecting too much.

An often lethal type of diarrhea has recently been found to be caused by one of the *Shigella* class of bacteria. It has not as yet been named. It produces almost the same symptoms as coccidiosis does. No drug has been found to cure it, but palliatives materially help the puppy to live. Constipating foods and rich foods all help.

Segregation is imperative. The puppies that seem well must be quickly taken away to uninfected places. The sick ones may be treated with any of the older remedies such as collodial, iodine, silver preparations, intestinal disinfectants and constipating foods, after a thorough initial physicking. None of the sulfas seems able to effect a cure, nor does penicillin. Strepto-mycin and Aureomycin have now been tried with considerable success in cases of diarrhea in older pups.

Food poisoning organisms are frequently found affecting little puppies, after they have eaten spoiled food, such as garbage. One litter was brought to our hospital showing pains and prostration. The puppy was given hydrogen peroxide, and it promptly vomited canned green string beans.

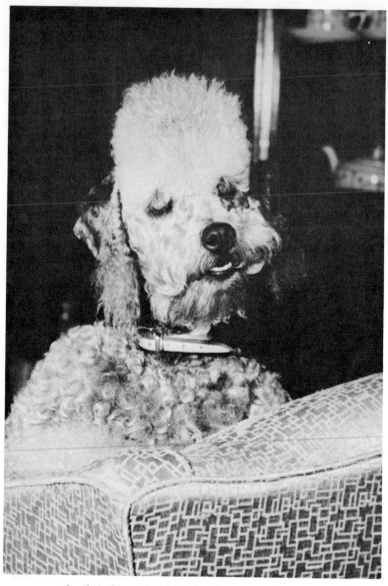

Caught in the act of winking, this Silver appears really coy.

Standards, Bel Tor St. Ay Better Mousetrap & Bel Tor Head Of The Class, Mrs. Jesse Mason, Bel Tor Kennels, Pine Orchard, Connecticut, owner.

POISONING

Poisoning is surprisingly rare in puppies, but you may know from experience that those energetic little animals will do crazy things if given the opportunity, lick spray material, eat paint, swallow soap, chew the top of an automobile battery, consume rat poison, roach poison, or an ant button. All these items, as many more, are poisonous and prompt treatment is necessary.

Symptoms. Pain, panting, trembling, vomiting and occasionally diarrhea are all symptoms of poisoning. The trouble is, of course, that they are symptoms of other ailments, too. You can usually make a definite diagnosis, though, by finding remains of the poisonous material or by knowing that your puppies had access to a source of poison.

Treatment. Call your veterinarian immediately. Be sure to let him know what poison the puppy ate if you know, before he leaves his office so that he may bring the proper antidotes. While he is coming, empty the puppy's stomach as quickly as possible. The best way to do this is to mix some peroxide of hydrogen, the drug usually called "peroxide", with an equal amount of water, and pour some down the puppy. Make him swallow it. A teaspoonful of the mixture will make a very small puppy vomit, while it may take 2 or 3 tablespoonfuls for a large puppy. He will vomit in about two minutes. Peroxide is an excellent antidote for phosphorus, which rat poison often contains. It is harmless, changing into water and oxygen when it fizzes.

Miniature, Crikora Calamity Jane, Wilbramont Kennels, North Wilbraham, Mass., owner.

If the puppy has eaten paint, as soon as his stomach is emptied and he stops vomiting, give a large pinch of Epsom salts, which is an antidote for lead poisoning and causes physicking as well. Leave further treatment up to the veterinarian.

PARASITIC DISEASES

With one exception, these have been considered in detail in the chapter on parasites. Because they produce disease symptoms, they are of great importance in themselves and must be treated in both mother and puppies (early in the life of the latter) and much hinges on this treatment. The only important parasitic disease which should be stressed now is *coccidiosis*. This is because coccidiosis usually occurs in puppies, at the earliest, when they start running around.

COCCIDIOSIS

There are three chief forms of the organism causing this disease in puppies and dogs, *Isospora begimina*, the smallest; *I. rivolta*, a middle-sized organism; and *I. felis*, which is the largest.

They seem to be harmful to puppies in the reverse order of their size, the smallest doing the greatest damage. *I. felis*, the cat form is found as often in dogs. The organisms or coccidia are so small they are almost in a class with bacteria. When they are passed out in stools in their infective form, they appear as you see them in the illustration. Sometimes the nucleus is doubled because of the first stage in cell division. The puppy becomes infected by getting some of these organisms into his mouth. As soon as they are ingested, they begin to change their forms and go through a cycle of changes. At one stage they possess a boring form and are able to bore through into the cells lining the intestine. There they multiply in enormous quantities, doing damage directly proportional to their numbers. The infectious form of the organism is then spewed out into the intestines and passed out in the stool. Your veterinarian can look at a sample of stool with his microscope and diagnose the presence of coccidia without guesswork.

The symptoms of coccidiosis are almost the same as those most people think of as distemper. About the only difference is that puppies do not shun light as they do in Carre distemper. The eyes fill with pus, the nose discharges, the temperature often goes to 104, the stools are fluid.

Treatment. Probably more medicines have been reported to cure coccidiosis than any other known disease. The cure notices continue to be circulated, but so far the truth seems to be that no known drug has the least effect on the disease. It improves of its own accord. Any drug which could kill the infecting organism would probably kill the tissue in which the organism lives. One drug tested was sulfaguanadine, and it proved, in safe doses, to be useless. In poultry, where heavy doses can be given, it has been shown to be effective though expensive, but such doses are harmful to puppies.

Miniature, Ch. Hermscrest Vaillantel, Mrs. F. M. Herma, Tarrytown, New York, owner.

VIRUS DISEASES

We very likely have not scratched the surface in our knowledge of the virus infections to which dogs and puppies are heir. Time was, not so long ago, when everything that made a dog sick was called "distemper." Now, in some sections, true distemper has almost ceased to be a problem and is one of the rarest of diseases. In other sections it still kills thousands of dogs annually.

Often litters of puppies have been brought into my hospital with diarrhea. Bacterial examination by competent bacteriologists show no pathogenic or disease producing bateria and no parasite eggs. Some of the puppies die, and some live. Chances are that an unknown virus disease has done its work. The whole field of such diseases offers a wonderful opportunity for study, although we do know something about some viruses and how to control them.

CARRE DISTEMPER

What was once called distemper, before vaccination became prevalent is now called Carre distemper in honor of the man who discovered that it was a virus-caused disease. Carre was the first to start unscrambling all the diseases of the "distemper complex."

Symptoms. Carre distemper was thought, some years ago, to be a disease of weaned puppies only, since it was held that puppies obtained some

Toy Silver, Lady Bug of Yewtree, Mrs. George Fiig, Johnstown, Pennsylvania, owner.

Toy, Macaulay White Cygnet, Nellie MacAulay, New York, New York, owner.

maternal immunity. Recent research however, shows us that four-week-old puppies often contract the disease. It is a question how little puppies would obtain immunity, especially if their mother had never had the disease. So it is of particular concern in cynidiatrics.

Differentiating or diagnosing the diseases of mature dogs is a very simple matter compared with doing the same thing for puppies. There are so many puppy diseases, each producing similar symptoms, and causing early death, that the very best specialist may make mistakes, especially if he is given only one opportunity to observe the puppy. Then, too, the puppies may die so quickly after being infected with a disease that there is no time for lesions to develop. In such cases, even a post-mortem examination is of no avail. When one has a litter to observe, the situation is different.

In small puppies, Carre distemper causes great prostration about the seventh day after the initial infection. Then follow running noses, mucous-filled eyes, dry hacking cough, loss of appetite, fever of 103 or over and loose stools, becoming darker as the disease progresses. The eyes become very sensitive to light and the puppies will try to remain in a dark or dim place blinking and squinting, if forced into the light. The younger the puppies, the higher the mortality rate.

Breeds differ greatly in their resistance. Some will survive in better than

Toy, Wayne Valley Excalibur. Wayne Valley Kennels, Corry, Pennsylvania, owner

a 50% proportion, while others, like Bloodhounds, will usually all die. Breeds vary in their symptoms also. The first observable symptoms of Carre distemper in Beagles are usually running fits. Cockers, as soon as the first rise in temperature occurs, seldom have fits. Poodles seldom have the fits either.

Treatment. If the disease breaks out in your litter of puppies, call the veterinarian at once. He will procure serum and inject every puppy with large amounts. Research has shown that the 10- and 15-cc doses which used to be given are generally useless in larger puppies. The longer the disease has progressed without treatment, the greater the amount of serum needed. Some large puppies need 100 cc. of serum to benefit. Laidlaw and Dunkin claimed better results with small doses, but our commercial serum, under practical field tests, has not shown enough value in small doses to warrant its use, in my estimation. Globulin, a component of serum, is coming to be used a great deal.

Once the disease has been aborted or prevented in your early infected puppies, you must not live in a fool's paradise. The protectiveness of the serum has not immunized your puppies for life. Laidlaw and Dunkin said that serum protected for 9 days. Therefore, after a large initial dose, it is quite necessary to administer small protective doses for many weeks. Then some time must elapse, during which protective substances furnished by the serum are lost before permanent immunization is practicable. Vaccine, if given too soon, is neutralized and little benefit is derived.

Prevention. We have been talking about treatment when distemper makes its dread appearance. Now, how can we prevent the disease?

There are at least 10 successful methods of immunization against Carre distemper. Some have more to recommend them than others. Some have distinct drawbacks. The most important factor to consider is the state of preservation of the biologics used. If they are fresh and have been kept at proper temperature, any of the ten methods listed below is satisfactory. The IF is a very large one.

Laidlaw and Dunkin's original method was the use of a dose of fresh vaccine followed in a week by a dose of live virus. But procuring live virus today is a gamble. Other research has shown that the virus is not at all necessary; that if enough fresh vaccine is given, one dose, graded to the size of the dog, will immunize him for life, or at least for many years. It is doubtful if any better method has yet been devised. Vaccine is safe, fairly certain, produces no ill effects, and is inexpensive.

The newest method is the use of live virus grown on hens' eggs. This is dried by a freezing method in a vacuum and reconstituted before use. This kind of virus, but called vaccine, is easily obtainable in a live, effective form. And it is an excellent method of vaccination.

Standard, Tory Hollow Tomahawk, Priscilla D. Baird, Berwyn, Pennsylvania, owner.

Toy, Ch. Fieldstream's Valentine, Mrs. Audrey W. Kelch, Peekskill, New York, owner.

Toy, Ch. Nibroc Gary, Mrs. Peter Frelinghuysen, Smilestone Kennels, Morristown, N. J., owner.

An expression which has come into vogue of late years is "puppy shots." This is a vague term usually referring to injections of serum. Possibly your veterinarian may favor them. I hope not, unless he is *sure* there is distemper in the neighborhood and flies are abundant. Flies spread the disease. If serum is given, then time must elapse for the effects to wear off before the puppy is in a condition to be vaccinated. Why should serum be given when vaccine could just as well be given starting permanent vaccination while the pup is, say, one month old? A week after such an inoculation the puppy is able to throw off the distemper virus. Even if he did contract it, he would have a very light case. Then later, if he has not been exposed and he is much larger, a full dose, graded to his size, can be given and he will be immunized for life.

The Green method has been much publicized and has considerable to recommend it. This method consists of injecting live virus collected from ferrets which have had the disease and attenuated or aged the virus. It is even claimed that the virus injected into dogs just starting with the disease will help bring about a cure. The Green method depends for its success partly on the fact that the virus is alive. If assurance can be given that it will be alive when injected, it should be a great boon because it can be used on puppies as well as grown dogs. If it is alive, it should cause the disease in a very mild form.

Silver Toy, Dracrest's Merri Minx, Anna M. Drake & Cora Swackhammer, Madison, New Jersey, owners.

If it is not alive, the dog owner does not know whether his dog has been successfully immunized or not.

METHODS OF SUCCESSFUL CARRE DISTEMPER IMMUNIZATION

1. Fresh vaccine alone, one dose, graded to the size of the puppy.
2. Vaccine, followed by live virus.
3. Vaccine, vaccine, and live virus.
4. Vaccine, followed by Green virus.
5. Serum and live virus, simultaneously given.
6. Serum and exposure to true Carre distemper.
7. Vaccine with dead complicating organisms.
8. Blood virus alone.
9. Vaccine followed by blood virus.
10. Green virus alone.

The author's preference is the first. The others are not given in the order of their value or of preference, but more or less in the order of their use as they have been developed.

INFECTIOUS HEPATITIS

This is the newest of the distemper complex diseases. It is caused by a virus which, in mature dogs, produces a mild disease. Every serious student of it has remarked that if a dog sick with hepatitis lives one day after the symptoms show up, he does not die of the disease. If he does die it is because of some other disease or a combination of diseases.

While this is true of mature dogs it is not so in the case of puppies which often die when they are in the early stages. Some die so soon that the disease has had no chance to leave any telltale marks.

Puppies which survive a few days 'show a thickened gall bladder, turn yellowish and if they survive often have the transparent front of the eyeball turn to a bluish color. Often only one eye is affected and in a few weeks this color changes back to normal.

Dogs which are sick can be helped by giving them glucose in such a form as corn syrup or powdered dextrose made into a thin syrup.

It seems advisable to have all puppies vaccinated against hepatitis while they are quite young. This, in the opinion of veterinarians of my acquaintance, will carry them long enough so that, if they should become infected later the disease wont amount to much and they will be immune for life.

There are vaccines now available which will immunize against three diseases at the same time.

Toy, Highland Sand Magic Toy, Highland Sand Kennels, Tucson, Arizona, owner.

PHARYNGO-LARYNGO-TRACHEITIS (P-L-T)

This is a relatively new disease, having been described in 1943 for the first time under the name of Housedog Disease. It often masquerades as Carre distemper, but the symptoms are sufficiently different to eliminate too much confusion.

The first symptom is a phlegmy cough as contrasted with the dry light cough of Carre distemper. The pup seems almost to be trying to raise something which is stuck in his throat. This cough can easily be confused with that exhibited when puppies are gagging up the larvae of round or hookworms, if they are heavily infested with worms. The temperature is low, staying between 102 and 103 and being predominantly 102.6 F. The stools become somewhat loose and the appetite diminishes, but to no such extent as in Carre's disease. The nose may run and the eyes fill somewhat, but neither of these symptoms are as pronounced as in the real distemper.

One of the really noticeable differences between Housedog Disease and Carre distemper is in the appetite. Once the throat phase of Housedog Disease is over, if encephalitis ensues, the dogs eat normally right up to the approach of death. They do not do this when affected with Carre distemper.

The younger the puppy is, the more likely he is to develop encephalitis.

Miniature, Touchstone Top Knick, Touchstone Kennels, Frederick Dyckman & Charles E. Knapp, Fishkill, New York, owners.

Standard, Chez Caniche's Napoleon, Mrs. Ada B. O'Donnell, Plymouth, Mass., owner.

In a series of dogs studied over a year, only 9% developed the brain symptoms, while in puppies under six months 36% developed them.

Pneumonia may follow the throat symptoms; and whether it does or not, the causative virus often invades the puppies' brains and causes encephalitis. This may take many forms although the most common are convulsions and twitches. The former may be no more than a slight frothing from the mouth, or it may be so violent that the puppy races about screaming and ends up in a tetanic convulsion which may last many minutes. These usually occur more and more frequently until the death of the pup. On the other hand, they may slacken and the puppy may appear to be recovering, only to start crying and slowly or suddenly to develop a twitch. The twitch may affect only one small muscle, a large muscle, or groups of muscles. Sedatives are indicated; your veterinarian will know best how to treat such a dog.

It is typically a disease of dogs kept indoors and so far seems to be confined almost entirely to the northeastern part of the United States.

INFLUENZA

Rare, except during outbreaks of severe influenza in human beings is this explosive disease. It sweeps through a kennel like Carre distemper. Puppies are prostrated with but little warning. They remain sick with fevers over 105F. for about 5 days and suddenly seem almost well again. Occasionally

Miniature, Ch. Crikora Commotion, Mrs. J. Donald Duncan, New York, New York, owner.

bacterial diseases follow. Pneumonia is a common one, but with protective drugs, you need not worry too much about that. Many cases in puppies and dogs were reported for two years when influenza ravaged humanity, but that type of influenza has not been seen since, to my knowledge.

A unique fact about the disease is that dogs having had it are not immune to Carre distemper, but dogs which have had distemper are immune to this influenza. This fact is another excellent reason for Carre distemper immunization.

BACTERIAL DISEASES

Leptospirosis. The principal form of this bacterial disease is called *Cavicola fever*. And here is a disease transmissible to human beings by dogs. It is contracted by us from dogs' excreta. It is much more common than people generally realize. In dogs it sometimes is mild. In man its symptoms may seem like influenza. Proper diagnosis from blood tests can only be made after the disease has subsided. If a person has a sick dog which is recovering, and that person becomes sick, the dog's blood may be the best means of diagnosing the disease. Prompt treatment with tetracycline effects a cure.

Dogs usually contract it from urine of other dogs. They may drink from a puddle with urine in it. Or they may jump into water where a sick dog has previously been. A dog sick with Cavicola fever may become jaundiced and some die but most recover and may be left with damaged kidneys and hearts which materially shorten their lives.

This is seldom a disease of puppies but puppies may be vaccinated successfully against it. Every dog should be, in the opinion of most veterinarians and physicians.

Sick dogs can be helped greatly by tetracyclines your veterinarian can supply, after he has made a diagnosis.

DEFICIENCY DISEASES

These are all due to inadequate diets. While puppies are nursing, if they have no parasites, they will come through to the age of weaning with no apparent deficiencies. It is after weaning that trouble develops. True, the iron and some other salts will have become dangerously low if no foods rich in them have been fed, but even then most puppies will seem to be in excellent health at weaning.

It is difficult to devise a formula that will be deficient in any single vitamin or mineral, especially when natural foods are fed. Consequently deficiency diseases are not common.

A deficiency of several of the vitamins results in a loss of appetite, in weakness, or in death. Making a diagnosis of vitamin deficiency requires a

Standard, Ch. Forzando The Imp Of Ivardon, Dr. William H. Ivens, Jr., Doylestown, Penna., owner.

very careful consideration of what has been fed the pup for several weeks. Vitamin deficiencies do not manifest themselves in a day. Some vitamins are stored and some are not, but most of them have to be deficient in a diet for several weeks before their absence is apparent.

It is impossible for either a layman or a veterinarian to look at a puppy that is very sick, won't eat and is getting ready to die and realize immediately that he hasn't been getting enough pantothenic acid. No veterinarian could, on the basis of one examination definitely ascribe a puppy's paralysis to a deficiency of biotin.

Vitamin A Deficiency. You have perhaps read that an eye disease, *xerophthalmia* is caused in puppies by a scarcity of Vitamin A. This is true, but don't jump to the conclusion that sore eyes in your puppy means that he needs cod-liver oil. Sore eyes can also be caused by infections and injuries. The kind that Vitamin A deficiency causes requires many days to show. It is an extreme symptom.

One result of a mild deficiency of Vitamin A is an upset in the cellular picture in the blood. The detection of this is a matter for specialists.

Vitamin A deficiency causes a loss of thrift; and, when the deficiency is serious, the affected puppy is rendered more liable to disease infection because the cells lining the nasal passages and other parts of the body fail to

Toy, Ch. Tydel's Dancing Girl, Mrs. Marguerite Tyson, Minden, Nevada, owner.

Toy, Norgate Too Spicey, Lorraine Rothstein, New York, New York, owner.

develop. Infertility, night blindness, deafness, loss of weight, stunted growth, incoordinated movements, unthrifty coat, and scaling skin may be seen in a dog deprived of the vitamin long enough.

Various estimates of the amount of Vitamin A needed by growing puppies show that the largest puppy needs about 7,500 units a day and smaller puppies much smaller amounts. We shall consider means of supplying it in the section on Vitamin D deficiency because the two so often go hand in hand. However, it cannot be repeated too often that if you are feeding a complete diet, you need not worry about any of the supplements mentioned here. They are needed only for puppies who have a demonstrated deficiency or are receiving an unnatural inadequate diet.

Vitamin D Deficiency. Vitamin D is a marrying agent which unites calcium and phosphorus into bone. The deficiency of it causes rickets (faulty bone development). The amount of Vitamin D which dogs need has been estimated at anywhere from five and a half units per pound for large dogs, up to 123 units. The reason for the differences is that some investigators used minimum amounts of calcium and phosphorus in the experimental diets, seeking to supply just the amount they thought the puppies needed. Other investigators furnished more. When far too much of these two elements are provided, the picture changes. In the summer time, when enough calcium

Standard, Clarion Demitasse, Jaronda Kennels, Ridgefield, Connecticut, owner.

Miniature, Ch. Estid Aristo, Col. Ernest E. Ferguson, Los Angeles, California, owner.

and phosphorus are provided in the diet, the puppy makes enough Vitamin D in his skin to provide for his needs. Some investigators feel however, that the very largest dogs need more than they can make, while others say it is doubtful. The studies were made in the dark.

Many of the best dog foods contain so much calcium and phosphorus that there is but little need for much Vitamin D to be added. Ground bone is one of the least expensive ingredients of dog food, so a considerable amount is generally used, providing abundant calcium and phosphorus. Besides, it supplies 24% protein. One of the leading brands of dog foods was found, upon analysis, to contain 6% calcium and 5% phosphorus, whereas some other foods used in studies contained only a fraction of each.

To insure enough Vitamin D in the diet you need to know the best sources of it. The sources of Vitamin D are generally rich in Vitamin A also, so let us consider them together.

Fish liver oils are very rich in both Vitamins A and D. However, the oil part is toxic if fed in large amounts, and the concentrated oils such as percomorph oil are much better buys anyway. Percomorph oil sells today in small amounts for about 75c per 10 cc. which furnishes 750,000 units of A and 8,000 units of D. In larger amounts it is considerably cheaper. Compare this with the best cod liver oil costing about $1.25 per pint. The pint furnishes

Toy, Pixdown Ditto, Prihim Kennels, Sinking Springs, Pennsylvania, owner.

about 400,000 units of A and 40,000 units of D, making the unit cost much greater than that of the A and D in percomorph oil. In fact, percomorph oil is probably the best and cheapest form in which to buy these vitamins.

Vitamin D alone may be bought least expensively in the form of irradiated yeast. The best commercial grade furnishes 900 units per gram. There are four grams in a level teaspoonful. In a level teaspoonful of cod liver oil, which meets U.S. standards, there are 400 units of D. If your dog required, say, 100 units of D per pound and weighed seventy-five pounds, one gram of irradiated yeast would furnish him all he could use. For the average dog, a small pinch is enough. Irradiated ergosterol and other products in which Vitamin D is found generally are not as good buys as the above.

Carotene is a favorite with some to supply Vitamin A. Each of its units splits into two units of the true vitamin in the animal's body, but even it is more expensive to use than percomorph oil.

When milk is supplied a puppy, especially in the summer time when cows are on grass, there is little need to worry about the Vitamin A supply.

Vitamin B Complex Deficiency. Lack of Vitamin B_1 (thiamin), B_2 (riboflavin) nicotinic acid, pantothenic acid, biotin, the filtrate factor W, and some others about which less is known, has been shown to be responsible for some symptoms of disease in puppies. There are three reasons for con-

142

sidering these vitamins as a group instead of separately:—they are usually found combined in nature; lack of only one of them is a rarity, and they are most effective in treatment when given as a group.

If your puppy, in the absence of any demonstrated disease, shows any of the following symptoms, his trouble may be ascribed to the lack of one or several of the B-complex vitamins. These symptoms are rather typical: digestive disorders, nervousness, irritability, redness and inflammation of the skin on the abdomen, insides of the legs, and the chest, loss of weight, ease of fatigue, staggering gait, paralysis and black tongue.

Some of these symptoms require a little amplification. The redness observed on the belly may come from many other things, especially external infection. Paralysis may also be due to other causes, but a lack of biotin is one of the causes when nutritional deficiency is to blame. Black tongue is a disease which does not turn the tongue black at all. Rather the tongue becomes inflamed and the mouth has a particularly obnoxious odor. After death the tongue may be so purple that it appears black.

Meat, organs, fish, egg yolk, yeast, whole grains and wheat germ are all rich in this group of essential vitamins. In the case of Vitamin B_1, fat in the diet exerts a very sparing effect. More B_1 should be fed when diets are low in fat, and less when they are richer.

Miniature, Ch. Tile Demi Tasse, Miss Laura Niles, Tilo Kennels, Bayshore, New York, owner.

Whether or not your puppies should be fed the complex depends upon the diet. If you are feeding a diet containing 5% wheat germ meal, 7% alfalfa, some yeast and some meat, there is no need for supplementation.

Heat destroys B_1 easily, and long exposure to heat is devastating to most of it. The canning process destroys a large percentage of vitamins; canners add much more vitamins than they expect the finished product to show, and the conscientious ones see that the final unitage is sufficient. Baking biscuits at great heat and long exposure destroys most of several of the B-complex vitamins. For this reason you must add B-complex supplements if you feed the baked products as certain biscuits or kibbled biscuits.

The Animal Growth Factor. For many years scientists suspected that there was something in animal protein which produced growth. The factor, when discovered, was called by many names. Finally it was learned that the element, *Cobalt*, was the key to this growth factor. Today nutritional scientists have a chemical name for it while laymen call it the animal protein factor, vitamin B_{12} or the animal growth factor.

It is essential to growth. If cobalt is present in the diet even in minute amounts mature dogs seem to make their own by the work of bacteria. Dogs fed meat, fish and byproducts of them, even in dry form obtains plenty of B_{12}.

Other Vitamin Deficiencies. Although mature dogs manufacture their

Toy, Calvinelle Wag Tag, Lillian E. Perry, Upper Marlboro, Maryland, owner.

Toy, Ch. Lime Crest Topper, Mrs. Robert D. Levy, Lime Crest Kennels, Miami, Florida, owner.

own Vitamin C, cases have been reported in which puppies seemed unable to do so and developed some of the symptoms of scurvy. Anemia, swelling of the jaw, and partial paralysis were reported by one investigator. Another found that his puppies were sensitive to pressure near the joints and wanted to lie down most of the time, as if standing pained them. Supplying a little orange or lemon juice cured them.

We have already mentioned the need of puppies for Vitamins E and K, and how both may be supplied in alfalfa leaf meal or in the form of wheat germ meal of Kayquinone, giving very small amounts a day. However, there is no evidence that the puppies require either vitamin as they get older. Both may be omitted when the diets given dogs contain wheat germ and alfalfa.

Mineral Deficiencies (Calcium and Phosphorus). We have discussed Vitamin D as a marrying agent of the calcium and phosphorus in the diet. Investigators have come to the conclusion that, when these minerals are present in only the minimum amounts necessary the ratio of calcium to phosphorus should be 6:5 for best assimilation; that is, one fifth more calcium than phosphorus. However, we do not hear much about the efficiency ration when the diet contains far more of both than is needed. Consider the dogs that you know that lived to old age on diets consisting mostly of bones. Aside from the constipation they experience, they are not harmed by the superfluity of these minerals.

Miniature, Ch. Icarus Duke Otto, Mrs. Robert Tranchin, Beajeu Kennels, Dallas, Texas, owner.

When manufacturers add bone meal to their formulas to help supply protein, they add more calcium and phosphorus than dogs can possibly use. Under such feeding regimes, rickets is almost unknown, even when small amounts of Vitamin D are added. On this basis, I suggest feeding more of these two minerals to your pups than they require. Apparently there is no harm and your worries about rickets are banished completely.

Iron. Iron is sometimes short in diets. When puppies are bled white by hookworms or are anemic from other causes, the addition of small amounts of ferrous iron does wonders in bringing them up to par. You may obtain it in the form that humans take and give it in proportion. Meat, either fresh or in the form of scraps, contains so much iron that if a diet is 10% meat scraps the puppies will have enough iron.

Other Minerals. Copper is necessary, but most foods have enough so that more need not be added in chemical form. Occasionally one sees a puppy respond to tiny amounts of magnesium, given as Epsom salts. On the whole, deficiencies of calcium, phosphorus and iron are far more prevalent than those of other metals.

Salt (Sodium and Chlorine). Manufacturers of dog and puppy foods usually see that their products contain 1% of salt. It is taken for granted that anyone preparing a diet for pups will flavor it by using a little salt. Milk

146

contains very little, and you should provide salt in the food of the pup. Wild animals get much salt from the blood of their prey. If you do not feed blood to your puppies, you must see that they are fed sodium and chlorine in the form in which you eat it.

Iodine. Iodine is an essential mineral, but most diets have enough. If bitches are starved of iodine, their puppies may be born deformed (cretins); and no puppy can thrive if all iodine is withheld from his diet. However, providing iodine is a simple proposition when natural foods are fed. They will have more or less iodine depending on where they are grown. If you add iodized salt to the food your puppies will get all the iodine they need.

Perhaps some of you may consider this advice about salt and iodine superfluous, but it is amazing how many dog breeders act surprised when their veterinarians ask them if they ever put any salt in their dogs' diet. They just never think of it.

Intussusceptions. A condition not infrequently found in puppies, but only rarely in grown dogs, is a telescoping of the bowel, known as an *intussusception*. The cause is not known, but it also occurs in children. An area of the intestine works inside and downward producing a swelling through which food cannot pass. If the condition is diagnosed early enough a veterinarian can remove a section of the intestine and join the sound ends, thus saving the life of the puppy.

Standard, Ch. Prankster Darius, Mrs. George Marmer, Prankster Kennels, Peabody, Mass., owner.

Frequently, after deworming, when too drastic physics are administered, a portion of the intestine folds inward and is pushed downward by the movements of the intestines. Gradually the fold moves along until congestion becomes so intense that it can move no further. The inside fold becomes dead and decomposes in some degree. The blood supply becomes pinched off because of the swelling. The puppy invariably dies unless surgery is resorted to.

Diagnosis is quite a simple matter. The first symptoms are vomiting, scant passages of feces and loss of appetite. Puppies have been known to live for three weeks after intussusception but they become thinner and thinner. It is generally possible and easy to palpate the abdomen. The sausage-shaped lump may be felt clearly. There is often some pain, and occasionally puppies hold the abdominal walls so tense that the thumb and fingers cannot feel through the stomach walls. Persistence will reward the examiner. Gradually the abdomen will become relaxed until the lump may be felt.

FITS

As in the case of diarrhea, fits are more often than not a symptom of some disease. They are actually convulsions, no matter how mild or how severe they may be. The convulsions may be caused by toxins or brain inflammation. Some of them resemble epilepsy in human beings and have apparently no

Black Toy, Cr. Fieldstream's Bojangles, Mrs. Audrey W. Kelch, Fieldstream Kennels, Peekskill, New York, owner.

Silver Toy, LaGae Beau's Fiddler, Mrs. Eva Blake, Caperlea Kennels, College Point, New York, owner.

ordinary cause. The following principal causes which I have noted in my work with dogs are listed in the order of their importance.

Encephalitis. Encephalitis easily ranks first. There probably is no real disease called encephalitis; rather it is the result of brain damage, generally by a virus of some other disease. The encephalitis which on rare occasions follows whooping cough or measles in children is caused by the virus of these diseases getting into the brain and inflaming it. You say that the child has the condition of encephalitis rather than the disease. When this condition follows P-L-T, the dog has it as a result of the P-L-T virus.

When a puppy develops encephalitis from any cause, it may have fits, although some never have fits. When a dog or puppy is brought to the Whitney Veterinarian Clinic, with a temperature in the vicinity of 102.6F we naturally suspect encephalitis, due to the common P-L-T virus, and make tests to show if this disease is present or not.

Kibbled Dog Food used to rank second as a cause of fits. The agene bleach used in some batches of kibbled dog foods produced fits in a positive manner. We have often tested such foods. I have seen young dogs have fits after being fed kibbled biscuits for no more than three days. Bakers are now leaving the agene out of foods and bleaching flour with other chemicals.

Deficiencies in kibbled dog food may be another cause of fits. Baking foods

Could be identical twins. This evenly matched pair of Miniatures in Dutch Clip present a striking appearance.

at the high temperature to which biscuits are subjected for long periods of time cannot help but result in some losses of essential nutriments.

The texture of kibbled biscuits and whole biscuits, which fill stomachs of puppies, often produces fits. Many a time we have had little puppies in violent fits rushed to us. Their stomachs have been emptied of loads of kibbles and their fits stopped at once. Many people who feed dog biscuits often do not soak them long enough.

Combinations of causes sometimes produce fits when kibbles are fed. The positive cause coupled with deficiencies is just too much for many puppies.

Parasitic infestation may cause convulsions in puppies. Hookworms, roundworms and tapeworms are the offenders in younger puppies, but whipworms come into the picture as the dogs grow older. Occasionally a puppy affected with coccidiosis has fits. Four instances of fits after a severe case of coccidiosis have come to this author's attention. The felis form of coccidia was not involved in any. Each of the puppies acted as though the seizures were virus fits, but examinations of their brains by a competent pathologist revealed the presence of coccidia.

Temperature fits are quite common. They are a frequent early symptom of Carre distemper among certain breeds, though less frequent in others.

150

High temperatures due to influenza and to pneumonia have been reported as causes, and high temperatures accompanying other diseases bring about the conditions propitious for fits.

Autointoxication due to intestinal impactions (stoppages) which in turn may be accounted for by food masses or foreign bodies, ranks as one of the positive causes of convulsions. Simple enemas often cure these impactions and subsequent regulation of elimination works wonders.

Foreign bodies in the stomach produce such pains that they lead any casual observer to believe the puppy has a fit, and often they do actually produce the real thing. Among the objects positively known to have been the direct cause of the upset which I have removed from puppy stomachs are four iron jacks, the porcelain part of a spark plug, a 10-inch knitting needle, many lumps of coal, small stones (in one case a puppy had four ounces of pebbles in his stomach), wads of grass, wads of hay, bones, sausage casings, half a rag doll, and a lump of tissue paper. Generally the worst fits are caused by hard objects.

Teething can cause fits. It must have done so much more frequently in the past than it does now, because most of the old books on dog diseases have paragraphs on teething fits and talk about them as if they were among the commonest of all puppy ills.

Standard, Chenue De La Fontaine, Dr. & Mrs. A. Stehr, Saulte St. Marie, Ontario, Can., owner.

Canadian & American Ch. The King's Jester of Encore, Mrs. Jane Fitts, Encore Poodles, Palmetto, Georgia, owner.

SKIN DISEASES

Puppies are subject quite early in life to many forms of skin disease, the majority of which are of fungous origin. A whole book could be written on this single subject. Some of the early treatises tell us that most of the puppy skin diseases are either moist or dry eczema, but recent research shows that this is untrue. The old idea of eczema was that the blood was of improper composition and the skin disease "boiled out." We used to read that certain foods were "too heatening to the blood," as if such a thing were possible. It may make you smile now, but our forefathers were very much interested in the "blood heatening" idea. Then, too, we were told that the puppies were exhibiting allergies or idiosyncrasies to the first solid foods, or even to the mother's milk.

It is obvious that if a skin disease can be cured externally with no change in the diet, the food is not responsible. If curing skin disease were as simple a matter as changing the diet, there would be very little to it. But recall, if you can, any case in which a skin disease was cured by changing the diet, and without the application of some local medicinal agent. If it was ever done, it was such a rarity that it may be explainable by causes other than change of food. For instance, cold weather will often cure skin diseases which thrive in summer. In all my experience in the handling of many thousands of dogs, I have yet to see the first dog that was affected with skin trouble which was caused by any positive ingredient in the diet. In our hospital during 1946 we treated over 2,000 cases of skin diseases. Not one was caused by any food.

There are some kinds of skin disease which are caused by vitamin deficiencies, but they are not the kind that you are likely to see if you are feeding an ordinary diet. Very severe infestations of intestinal parasites can cause coat effects, which disappear when nothing else is done than to deworm the dogs.

152

How some Poodles look before grooming.

The common puppy skin diseases are generally infections, and can be cured by external applications of remedies which your veterinarian will recommend. Often they get their start from flea and louse bites. I have done considerable research using mixtures of flea-destroying drugs and fungicides and find that it is possible to keep dogs freer from skin disease when combinations of the two are used than when one is used alone.

All through his life every dog is subject to skin disease, especially when the weather is moist and hot. Fungous disorders spread best under these conditions and bathing is one of the best ways to spread such afflictions. Puppies with small spots, easily controllable if treated early will become infected all over their bodies if given baths. They must be cured first, even though they do give off offensive odors during the curative stages. There are few effective fungicides which work well in water bases unless they are applied several times a day. Oil bases or soap are best; therefore the diseases should be cured before the dog is washed.

The earliest skin disease is generally a rash on the belly, which soon spreads all over the body. But as the puppy grows, the more prevalent types are those which first start on the back in front of the tail.

Many, if not most of the diseases affecting older dogs also cause sicknesses in puppies, but abnormal growths like cancer are seldom found and kidney disease is rare, as are diseases of the urinary tract, paralysis, and certain eye disorders.

Rabies is common in puppies but not as much so as among older dogs, especially those which roam. Puppies haven't learned or felt the urge to roam. In states where rabies is prevalent all puppies should be vaccinated against it. Once-a-year vaccinations will usually prevent rabies effectively throughout the life of the dog.

X
Parasites

Internal and external parasites must be diligently eliminated if puppies are to thrive. In order to know how to take care of these pests, one has to know at least a little about their life histories.

ROUNDWORMS

While not so severe a tax as some parasites which puppies harbor, roundworms do untold damage in the aggregate. They account for the deaths of thousands of puppies annually. The puppies die not only because the worms are in the stomach and intestines, but because of lung infestation which leads to pneumonia. How does this situation come to be?

A puppy gets a roundworm egg in its mouth. The egg may be ingested from the mother's teats, fur or feet. Or it may be picked up from a bone which the mother has dragged around in her run and brought into the puppy box. Or, if the puppies are old enough, the worm egg may have been picked up directly by the mouth from the ground or possibly have been blown in dust onto food which the pup then eats. However, after the egg reaches his mouth, here is what happens: It is swallowed. It has a tough coat or shell, so resistant that it will live in the soil for years and stand soaking in some disinfectants, but when the acids of the stomach attack it, the shell is dissolved and the little worm within the shell is liberated. In this form it is the *larva*. The tiny, microscopic thing is moved into the intestine and at once it bores through the intestinal lining until it gets into the blood or lymph, by which route it enters the general circulation.

It floats about in the blood stream until, after further development, it ends up in the lungs, and there it bores through from the blood side of the lungs to the air side. It causes irritation and, as it moves and is moved upward from the lungs to the throat, produces the cough characteristic of heavy infestation. One lonesome larva probably would have little effect, but large numbers of them cause great irritation and often pneumonia, as they damage the lungs.

The larva is finally gagged up into the throat and is promptly swallowed. Now it grows to adulthood and lives in the stomach or intestine the rest of its life, migrating up and down so as not to be too close to other roundworms, except at mating time. When mating time arrives, male and female copulate, and the fertilized female lays great numbers of eggs which are passed out of the puppy with the feces, and if not cleaned up, may become scattered and infest the premises. Rain is especially helpful in scattering feces and washing

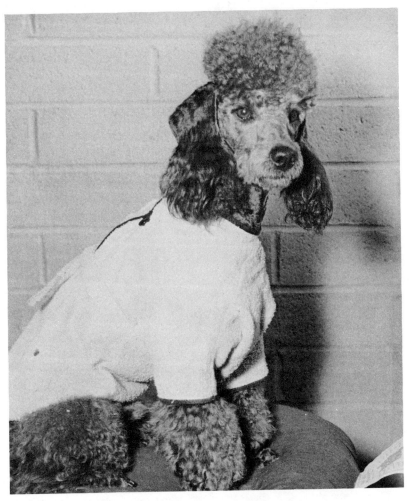

Henri in his Christmas bathrobe.

the eggs which are passed out of the puppy with the feces and washing the eggs into the ground. Here they incubate for considerable time, the period depending upon the temperature and amount of humidity.

A roundworm egg is not infestive until incubation has occurred. For this reason bitches can keep their puppies clean, sometimes consuming thousands of eggs daily along with feces ingested in the process of cleaning the puppies, and yet not become infested themselves. The eggs pass through her and are left in her stool. The incubation period is nearly a week whereas the eggs are in the bitch's body not more than 24 hours.

An aristocrat among dogs. This Poodle poses for his picture in a pet shop.

There, in a nutshell is the life history of the roundworm. There are two general kinds which may infest your puppies, but both have more or less similar life histories. Both are characteristically parasites of puppies and young dogs. As dogs get older, they seem to develop an immunity to this type of worm so that one finds very few roundworm eggs in the feces of adult dogs.

HOOKWORMS

In some respects the life cycle of the hookworm and that of the roundworm are similar. This is principally due to the fact that both spend part of their embryonic stage in the blood.

Hookworms are not harmful as eggs because the eggs are not infestive. After the egg appears in the puppy's stool, it hatches, if the temperature and moisture are both correct for their development, and the larval form goes

Silver Standard, Ch. Donna of Westford Ho, Harmo Kennels, Amherst, New Hampshire, owner.

through five pupations before it finally is infestive. Then it is usually ingested, although it is believed to be able to bore through the skin and the toes. When it reaches the intestine, it works itself through the intestinal lining and becomes a blood parasite.

By whatever way it gains admission to the blood, it finally arrives at the lungs, is coughed up and swallowed, and attaches itself to the intestinal lining by the hooks at its mouth (these hooks are responsible for its name). It lives by sucking blood. One hookworm can draw about a thimbleful of blood from a puppy in a week, so you can see why very early recognition is imperative if you are to save your litter or infested puppies.

While in the blood of a bitch, the larvae can and do bore through the uterine wall into the placenta and are carried to the puppy's body where they lie dormant until birth. But at birth they immediately start developing; the larvae do not have to go through the entire cycle as they do in older dogs which pick up the larvae themselves. This is the reason your puppies may show hookworm eggs in their stools as early as at two weeks of age. If they were to pick them up in their mouths, it would be three weeks before they exhibited eggs in their stools.

WHIPWORMS

These little parasites are about half an inch long in their body parts but have a long protrusion or flagella from their front ends which gives them the appearance of a whip. The flagella is about $1\frac{1}{2}$ inches long and is sewed into the intestinal lining to act as the means of holding on. A favorite place for whipworms is the cecum, a blind gut arrangement located at the upper end of the large intestine. There was a time when whipworms presented a problem in elimination, and operations were performed to remove the infested dog's cecum, but this is never necessary any more.

The whipworm egg is believed to require 20 days for incubation at optimum heat and moisture conditions. Like the roundworm egg, it is resistant. Once it is ingested and its shell removed, the little larvae are believed to become attached to the intestine without spending any time in the blood of the dog.

You will rarely find puppies with whipworms in the first few weeks of life.

TAPEWORMS

The tapeworm most commonly found in young puppies is the type whose intermediate host is the dog flea. The second most common one is that which has the rabbit as its intermediate host.

The flea type's life history is as follows: The puppy eats a flea in whose body is a tapeworm head enclosed in a cyst. When the flea is partially digested, the tapeworm head is liberated. It adheres to the intestinal lining by suckers which hold it there throughout its life. This microscopic head section grows and from it an extension develops. On the tail of this extension, another is added. To this another is added, and so on, the worm becoming longer and longer. Each addition, known as a segment or proglottid, puts a strain on the segments above it. When the worm is finally developed, the segments closest to the head have been pulled out by the strain upon them until they look like a long thread. Naturally, the closer the segments are to the tail end, the fatter they are.

These last segments become filled with eggs after the tapeworm has mated. It is interesting to note that one segment on the same worm may be male and another female so that the worm can often mate with itself, by twisting around and letting the lower segments touch those higher up.

The segments at the end with their ripened eggs, which when seen with a microscope, appear like bunches of grapes surrounded by a thin envelope, drop off. They may be found crawling out of the puppy's anus, on his bed, or sometimes clinging to the hair under his tail, dried and looking like small grains of brown rice.

The larval form of the flea, a worm, feeds on these segments and finds much nourishment in them. In consuming the meat of the segment, the larvae ingest the eggs which, as we have seen, become cysts in their bodies. Then the flea larvae spin cocoons where they pupate, and from each one of them a little flea emerges, containing within its body the head of a tapeworm. The fleas crawl into the mouths of puppies or grown dogs, and the cycle starts all over again.

In less than three weeks after an infested flea is swallowed by your puppy, you can find tapeworm segments on or in the stools of that puppy. These segments hold the eggs quite well, and it is exceptional to find eggs from the flea tapeworm in a dog's stool unless one of the segments happens to be mashed. Diagnosis can be easily made by seeing the segments on the stool or around the anus.

The rabbit-host tapeworm has a different life history. A dog with the worms in his intestine defecates where there is grass. Some of the eggs from the tapeworm (this type lays eggs) sticks to the grass and the blades grow up, carrying the eggs with it. An unsuspecting rabbit eats the blade of grass and the egg. The egg contains the larval worm which, unlike the flea-host worm larva, gets into the blood and eventually ends up in the liver as a favorite spot. Here the rabbit's body forms a cyst about it, and it lives within the cyst until the rabbit is shot, skinned and its liver fed by an unsuspecting hunter to his dog. The liver is digested, but not the worm, and it promptly attaches itself to the intestine and grows many segments, each somewhat fatter and larger than those of the flea-host tapeworm.

Then the eggs are laid and pass out in the feces, and segments of the worm also drop off where they are pushed around in the intestine and eggs mashed out of them. The presence of these worms may be determined both by the segments on the stool and eggs in the stool, which may be found with a microscope.

HOW THE PRESENCE OF WORMS IS DETERMINED

So many people appear to think that all they have to do to see if a puppy has worms is to look at the stool. Once in a while you may see roundworms which have died of old age and been expelled, or eliminated in some other way. They are about four inches long in adult form and easily seen, but because you do not see them, don't think that your puppies are free of them. Most puppies have worms. The only safe and sure way of determining their presence is by finding their eggs in the stool with the aid of a microscope. They must be magnified by over 100 times their real size to do a very good job of diagnosis.

Hookworms are so small very few people would know one if they saw it.

A white puppy
benched and
waiting to be shown.

Many think that tapeworm segments are hookworms or "pinworms." Most people seem to think that because worms are curled up at both ends they are hookworms. Most roundworms are curled up in this fashion. Very young roundworms often pass for hookworms in the eyes of many amateurs. Whipworms are very seldom seen even after a thorough worming because dog owners don't take the trouble to wash the stool apart over a fine screen to find them.

Tapeworm segments take so many forms that it is no wonder they are confusing to the amateur. Some will have shortened up to about an eighth inch square, others will elongate until they seem to have little heads, some will be pink, some yellow and some white, with all shapes and sizes in between. And when they are dry, as I have said, they shrink and harden so they look like little rice grains. So do not expect to see all forms of worms, and don't expect your veterinarian to find eggs of the flea-host tapeworm if he makes a fecal examination. He may see the segments in the stool and yet not be able to find a single egg. You can tell that they are there and help him.

THE LOUSE

Large numbers of puppies die every year because of louse infestation. If a bitch is infested as soon as she whelps most of the lice will leave her and attach themselves to the pups. The pups soon take on an untidy appearance and gradually develop a boardy feeling. It is amazing how many people have puppies infested this way and never think of looking closely enough to find the cause of the loss of puppy condition. I have seen experienced kennel men have a litter infested with lice and not know what was wrong. In fact, it is such a common experience for veterinarians to find well-kept dogs heavily infested that one wonders why.

Miniature Apricot, Ch. Meisen Golden Gaite, Hilda Meisen-gahl, Meisen Poodles, North Hollywood, Calif., owner.

A louse lays its eggs and sticks them to the hair of the dog. The eggs hatch and the little lice go to the skin, and, depending on whether they are the sucking or biting variety, stay put or move around sluggishly. They will be found nearly anywhere on the young puppy but on older dogs they tend to like the ears best, especially in long haired dogs. One should inspect every pregnant bitch for nits (the eggs) well before time of whelping, and see that they are removed by dipping her, or powdering her with a harmless potent louse powder. It is well, too, to remove the nits with any one of the solutions sold for the purpose.

It is the opinion of many that dogs pick up lice from their premises, and that they can live for long periods off the dog, but it is more likely that they pick up the lice from other dogs, and that lice live no more than three days off their host.

A large number of lice will make a puppy exceedingly anemic and cause death early in life. I have had to resort to transfusions to save several such puppies and transfusions in such young pups are difficult indeed.

FLEAS

Fleas, unlike lice, do not develop on the dog, and for this reason your puppy is not very likely to pick up fleas from another dog. The adult fleas ride around on the dog, mating and the females laying eggs, while they eat to their heart's content. The female fleas, when full of eggs, can be recognized by the huge yellowish or brownish abdomens, which make them look very different from the lithe and graceful high jumping males. The female fleas lay their eggs and rely on the travels of the dog to scatter them. That's why, although you keep your dog as free of fleas as you are yourself, a neighbor's flea-covered dog may stay around your house and yard, leaving thousands of flea eggs behind him.

If your puppy or dog has fleas and you keep him in the house, you can be sure he will leave eggs all over your house. There they will stay as long as it is dry and cold, but let a nice damp warm day come in early summer and all those eggs hatch out. Each occupant emerges as a tiny worm, eats organic matter, and grows until it is quite visible. Just before it pupates, it may be seen as a little brown and black worm, slightly more than an eighth inch long, moving about in cracks in the floor or maybe even in the tufts of the best overstuffed chair.

Worms spin cocoons and stay in them for several days, then they emerge as fleas, just as butterflies come from cocoons spun by caterpillars. At this stage the male and female fleas look alike, and both can jump prodigious distances. They climb on anything upright and jump for the first thing that goes past. My lady's calf, or the mother of the pups. If enough get on the bitch and she lies down with her pups, they will crawl off onto the pups and chew on them, producing little spots where skin disease can find a place of access.

You can easily control fleas by using good flea powders or by dipping your puppy in rotenone dips. D.D.T., properly used, is also effective and safe.

TICKS

In some sections of the world, ticks are a very serious problem, but they are rare in young puppies, unless the house in which the puppies are kept is infested. For this reason we shall not take the time to discuss their life history. Most dogs become infested by running outside in brushy country; seldom do the ticks let go their holds on the mothers and attach to the puppies. They can be eliminated by dips containing rotenone, or by being pulled out of the dog's skin with tweezers. Be sure to pull the head out if possible.

MANGE

Three forms of mange caused by tiny mites often affect dogs. They are as follows:

Sarcoptic. This is the form of mange that is caused by a roundish parasite, too small to be seen without magnification, which bores or tunnels through the skin. The disease spreads to human skin and back to animals.

Sarcoptic mange may appear anywhere on the puppy's body. Small points of infection appear as red spots somewhat raised, like little mounds. These spread and become continuous with the next until the skin shows large areas of reddish, thickened skin. Constant scratching inflames the areas so that the combination of internal and external irritation leaves the skin in a pitiful condition. There is often some moisture if the inflammation is very severe. Your veterinarian can give you medicine which will quickly eradicate mange from your puppies, but be sure that you yourself are not infested and spreading the parasite to the dogs. There is no disgrace in getting any kind of parasite; the disgrace is in keeping it. If you have a skin condition resembling mange, and you know your puppies have sarcoptic mange, tell your doctor about it. The information will help both him and you, as it may make it unnecessary to do painful skin scraping from one of your own affected areas.

Demodectic. Often called *red mange*, this is the skin affliction that used to be considered incurable. With the discovery of the effectiveness of rotenone, it now is among the simplest skin diseases to cure, but it is an insidious disease because the incubation period of the causative mites is so prolonged.

The cigar-shaped mite gets into the hair follicles and reproduces there, and young mites spread to other follicles. They are so small and require so much time to reproduce and grow that many weeks pass before they show on the dog's skin. When they do show, the first indication is a spot of thinned hair, not entirely bald. This more often than not occurs on the face, somewhere around the eyes, or on the front legs. There are, of course, exceptions, but certainly 75% of all cases show up first in these areas. There is no serious escape of fluid, but just a harmless looking baldish spot. This spot may be soon cured with medicine which you can obtain from your veterinarian, but meanwhile, in many other spots on the puppy, incubation is proceeding. The next thing you know, there are a dozen or so larger areas where the hair is coarser.

Dogs are often brought to our clinic with nine-tenths of their bodies nude, but they are curable even in such a condition. It takes some time to do it, and usually a month elapses before the hair returns. If your puppy has suffered from demodectic mange, your must keep everlastingly on the watch for the reappearance of new spots and treat them early.

Ear Mange. The mite which causes this painful and irritating condition is roundish in shape like the sarcoptic mange mite. It, too, is very small. It generally creates a greyish, dry type of wax in dog's ears, which is quite different from the sticky black wax of canker; also the odor from the ears is different from that produced by canker disease. Microscopic examination of the wax reveals eggs and mites of all sizes and conditions.

Since it takes several weeks for a few mites in the ear to reproduce enough to be irritating, this disease is a slow starter. Your veterinarian can show you what the mites look like when he examines the ear scraping. Very weak solutions of rotenone cause their death and prove effective, but the solution must be put around the outside, as well as inside the ear. I have found them close to the outside of the ear. Your veterinarian will show you how to apply the solution he gives you.

MISINFORMATION CONCERNING WORMS

It would hardly seem necessary, but in view of the fact that so many people have such fantastic notions of where worms come from, something must be said regarding the places worms do *not* come from.

Somehow the notion has become widespread that milk causes worms. It isn't quite as prevalent as it was, but it still is believed by thousands. If milk caused worms, why would doctors recommend that children be fed it ? I often ask that question, and some of my clients say that they have heard that it is not milk itself which causes worms, but that milk helps them to develop. This is like saying that milk is such a good food that worms also thrive in it as an environment. That might be so. But no puppy should be allowed to harbor worms. There is no known parasite of dogs that comes from milk, because *milk does not contain worm eggs.*

Some people believe that meat causes worms. As we have seen, feeding raw rabbit livers to dogs may cause the rabbit-host tapeworm. Occasionally feeding raw beef or raw pork will cause the beef-host or hog-host tapeworms, but I can assure you that these are great rarities in dogs. Feeding raw pork or undercooked pork to dogs or puppies can produce trichinosis in them just as it can in us, if the pork was obtained from hogs harboring the trichina worm.

From a practical point of view, it can be said that it is safe for you to feed raw beef because the chances of your dogs catching tapeworms from it are very slight; it is better not to feed raw pork. Pork loses very little food value in the cooking process and any trichina worms present are thereby destroyed. Even though beef and horsemeat also lose little food value when cooked, you have little reason to cook them for your dogs in the hope of preventing parasites.

Perhaps you have heard, too, that meat tends to help keep some parasites in check. It has been found that hookworms seem to do more harm to puppies when they have inadequate amounts of proper proteins than when they have enough. The meat can be raw, cooked, or dehydrated. Meat provides proteins and to that extent reduces parasitic damage.

Another superstition regarding worms is that garlic will act to remove them. This idea is given constant bolstering by the people who sell it. We do not see it advertised for the purpose because no substantial research has shown that it has value. But somebody at one time fed garlic and his puppy passed some worms. That person never bothered to ask whether the pup might not have passed the worms had he not been fed the garlic, nor did he bother to have a fecal examination made to determine whether there were still worms in the puppies. Dogs and puppies are brought to us which sometimes smell almost like a garlic bulb. We see many attempts at deworming with garlic. The very puppies that smell so strongly of it often will be among the worst infested animals. This is usually because the owners haven't bothered to try efficient worm-expelling drugs but depend on garlic, which is not very useful.

DEWORMING

A debatable question which interests both the veterinarian and the layman is: "Shall the dogbreeder deworm his puppies himself?" Some veterinarians will say "NO, NEVER!" Others will say, "Of course they should. I give my clients the medicine to take home and deworm their puppies every time I can."

Some dog owners will say, "NO, NEVER." They will go on to tell you of disastrous experiences they have had in doing it at home themselves. Others will tell you how they have been deworming their puppies for years and have never had one single bad experience.

The United States Department of Agriculture, largest employer of veterinarians in the world (the Bureau of Animal Industry employs thousands) believes that the dog breeder is capable of deworming his own puppies and dogs. It publishes a folder telling anyone how to do it. The department also believes that the layman is interested in understanding the diseases of his pets, and to encourage and assist him in this interest, it circulates a folder on the diseases of the dog. In the 1942 *Yearbook of Agriculture*, it published a fine chapter on "The Diseases of Dogs."

And to cap the climax, the U.S.D.A. developed and tested an anthelmintic (worm killer), normal butyl chloride, which was shown to be safe and useful. Today, in every corner drugstore across America, you can buy this drug, put up under different trade names by concerns which sell remedies for dogs. That the drug is safe has been attested by the Pure Food and Drug Administration of our government. It is effective against round-, hook-, and whipworms, but must be given in very large doses for whipworms.

From what I have said so far, you might conclude that I believe that there is no place for the veterinarian in the deworming of puppies, but this is not the case. We see the advantages and disadvantages of home treatments.

Approaching the problem strictly from the dog breeders' point of view, my opinion is that it is more than worth the price of a visit to, or from, your veterinarian to have the job done properly.

Without his assistance, you don't know what kinds of parasites your puppies have. Therefore, you don't know what kinds of medicine to use. You may decide on the basis of finding a few tapeworm segments, that your puppies have roundworms or hookworms. You give them medicine to eliminate these pests, but for some reason they get no better and continue to pass segments. Wouldn't it have been better if your veterinarian had made an examination and prescribed for them?

Again, you may assume that your unthrifty, anemic puppies have worms when actually they may be suffering from some disease. Many clients bring puppies to us who are ailing not from worms but from a severe case of coccidiosis. On the other hand, you may think that your puppies have a disease when they really have a severe worm infestation. Only your veterinarian can tell you definitely what the trouble is.

165

You may occasionally see your puppies sliding on their tails, and a helpful neighbor or a statement in a "dog book" will assure you that this is a positive sign of worms. On the contrary, it is usually a sign that the two glands located just under the anus are filled and irritating the puppies. Your veterinarian can probably tell you many amusing stories of how his clients have been mistaken as to the cause of this symptom. He squeezes the glands properly and expresses the acrid-smelling fluid out onto a piece of cotton, with which he covers his hand, showing that it was not worms that caused the irritation at all. He explains that severe roundworms infestations sometimes will produce sufficient toxin possibly to be the cause of this dragging or "playing sleighride" but that in many cases the accumulation of substance in the glands is what caused you to think the puppies have worms.

We have had hundreds of puppy raisers bring us feces and we soon learn the facts about their worms, give them the medicine and explain explicitly how to administer it. And even then one will occasionally phone to say one of the puppies was sick, but the owner found later that it had gotten to the cat's milk, or that the mother had jumped into the pen and one of the puppies nursed. So we advise leaving the puppies with us, if there is any chance that instructions cannot be properly carried out.

It is easy to see how the veterinarian comes to regard some clients with suspicion until he knows he can trust them to follow instructions. Looking at it from his point of view, can you blame him when some clients will bring back capsules and say, "The medicine was no good. You said on the directions, give both capsules, etc., etc., but the puppies refused to take them." That often happens.

Or take the case where the medicine did not work, and possibly made the puppy "drunk." The veterinarian makes inquiry and finds that the puppies were given all the milk they wanted, even though the instructions say to *starve*, underlined, for 24 hours. The client says, "But milk isn't food; milk is like water."

Some veterinarians maintain a mail diagnosis service. For trusted clients too far away to conveniently visit them, small receptacles are provided which may be filled and mailed. Careful studies are made, diagnosis is reported and the proper medicine sent for puppies whose weights are known. One southern veterinarian told the author that most of his fecal examinations are made on this basis. It is well worth the money for any dog breeder to know what kinds of worms his dogs harbor and know that the correct medicine is being given, in the correct amounts.

DEWORMING LITTLE PUPPIES

How young may a puppy be dewormed? This depends on the drug that is used. Wormseed oil and normal butyl chloride are somewhat more toxic to little puppies than tetrachlorethylene. Research indicates that even a week-old puppy may be safely treated but puppies that young do not have worms. At three weeks, there is little danger in deworming reasonably healthy infested puppies with tetrachlorethylene, provided they are starved for at least 20 hours. The drug may safely be given at the rate of 0.1 cc. for each 12 ounces of the puppy's weight.

One of the worst pieces of advice that can be given to the owner of a litter of heavily infested puppies is, "Don't deworm them until you have built them up." I have seen one fancier advise another in this way time after time, and then had the breeder consult us after the puppies were too far gone for help. You can't deworm them too soon; you usually don't have time to build them up because it is the worms that are debilitating them. Don't wait another minute to start starving them for the process.

It is often said to be advisable to give a little glucose before deworming. I find this unnecessary and have found no better results with it than without it, because I have never seen any harm come to a litter if they are thoroughly starved. Remember that tetrachlorethylene is soluble in fat. It is by the absorption of fat carrying the drug that the dog gets it from his intestines. If there is no fat, he gets very little of it.

But he does get some with or without glucose. Here is a nice little thing to know: After a litter of puppies has been wormed, in about half an hour you can smell the ether-like odor of the drug on the puppies' breath. Suppose you deworm 10 puppies which are all badly in need of it, and later on you find a capsule in the pen and realize that one of the puppies has spat it out or regurgitated it. How are you going to tell which one lost it? Just hold the nose of each one close to your nose and gently inhale. If you find one without an ether odor on his breath, you have located the pup you want and can see that he gets his medicine.

Puppies won't lose a capsule if it is pushed down the throat far enough. Drop the capsule on the back of the tongue and follow it down the throat with your finger as far as you can push. If it gets over the pharynx, and you see the puppy make a swallowing motion, it won't come up.

Another method of deworming dogs and puppies for roundworms is to give piperazine with the food. This quite benign drug was first used for human infants to rid them of pin worms. In dogs it is used in several forms such as piperazine citrate. The animals do not object to the taste. Your veterinarian can supply you.

But do not depend on any form of piperazine to dislodge all kinds of intestinal parasites; it is effective only against roundworms, removes about half of the hookworms and none of the whips.

XI
Early Training

"As the twig is bent, so is the tree inclined" is only partly true in dog training. A tree, once it inclines, remains that way, but an animal's mind, once it gets untrained by a long period of non-use, can be re-educated nicely. It is amazing how quickly and well little puppies can be trained in useful ways in the first place.

The principles of early training are so vital that I have thought it worthwhile to call your attention to the most basic of them before proceeding any further.

Housebreaking is one of the main concerns. A puppy eliminates in response to the feel of what he stands on. If he first does so on the wire of a wire-bottomed pen, he will more than likely do so subsequently on the grating of a one-pipe furnace if he can fine ond. If he learns first on newspaper, he will try to find that, and if he learns on a clipped lawn, he will sense that your rug with the deepest nap is the proper place to relieve himself.

Breeders often raise pups in a pen the bottom of which is covered with straw. Is it any wonder, therefore, that a pup whose only strawy environment is his new dog house with its straw bottom will soil only that. To make the buyer realize that he is getting an easily housebroken dog, start your pups on newspaper, and explain to the prospective buyer how to housebreak. When the puppy, in his new home, has become accustomed to using the paper spread on the kitchen floor, explain how it must be moved by stages out on to the back lawn or wherever it is desired to have the dog eliminate, how the pup should be taken out after meals when it normally feels the urge, and how the whole thing is a matter of habit formation, that the exceptions are serious, and how, if a puppy be given the opportunity he needs, there will be few failures.

Prospective buyers admire the response of young puppies to commands. You can teach them what *go in the house* means, and to come to a whistle, the word *come*, or the clapping of your hands. Use words distinctly as you shoo them into their house, or when you call them out to feed them. It does not require very many repetitions of words to establish a conditioned reflex, and the word will have a meaning.

Only a minutely small percentage of dogs are ever field trained, but I feel sure that if more owners knew the fun they are missing by never giving their dogs a chance at their work, many dogs would be field trained. Even ten-week-old puppies will show interest. It pays well to be able to demonstrate

Housebreaking should begin at an early age. This puppy is learning to use newspapers for other than reading purposes.

these early aptitudes to prospective buyers. Only a few minutes a day need be spent in rolling a ball for puppies to chase and catch. Once they start this, it is easy to train them, one at a time, to drop the ball in your hand or at your feet.

At the tender age of four weeks every puppy in a litter can be standing like a rock in show position. Indeed this is the best age to start them. A connoisseur can make a fairly accurate appraisal of the best of any litter by this early posing and training and the pups enjoy it.

A small tidbit given at the conclusion of the posing session will help you establish the pattern. With one of your fingers under the puppy's jaw and another under his tail, the puppy will stand as if hypnotized for some minutes. Examine his mouth, and don't let him win should he resist your efforts. End each training period by showing him that you and your hands are much stronger than he is, and that you are boss.

I am often amazed at how ineffectual many people are. Almost unable, apparently to use their hands enough to force a puppy to their will, these persons will complain, "If I discipline him, he comes right at me and bites." Some dogs are thus trained to be ugly. Why, the weakest woman could easily kill a half-grown pup with her bare hands. Poor training cannot be excused by saying, "I can't." What it really means is, "I won't try."

Training the dog to *sit* on command and to *stay* when ordered to do so.

A puppy which is made to submit to human beings, and which acknowledges early in his life that they are his superiors, will usually remain tractable throughout his existence, unless he possesses inherited meanness—an unreliable temperament. Even such puppies can be trained to be more reliable, but they should not be used for breeding.

TRAINING YOUR DOG

Now I realize, of course, that there are thousands of dog owners who have rationalized the dog up into the realm of the human being. You even read such statements by authors on dog training as, "The dog is not a seal, so don't feed him when you train." Many dog owners, especially those who have helped give dogs an evil reputation by spoiling their dogs until they have nasty dispositions, will tell you it is cruel to discipline a dog in any way except scolding.

Well, it is true that dogs can be trained without rewards by the system presently in vogue—the force system—and it is true that they can be trained without physical discipline. But just compare the efficiency of the methods and the effect on your dog of those outworn fifteenth-century methods with the new ones based on modern psychology. A dog isn't a seal; he may not be quite so bright as a seal, and he is definitely not of human mental caliber. So treat him and train him for what he is, and your rewards and pleasure from what you will learn yourself will be immeasurably increased.

It is necessary to capture the dog's attention and to be very firm in one's commands.

With the new methods you can train your pet in a tenth of the time most persons spend.

BASIC PRINCIPLES FOR TRAINING

We start out with the established fact that *a dog's behavior is never uncaused.* The brain receives impressions from the senses and reacts to them. The pattern of reaction depends in part on the dog's inheritance. As we have observed in Chapter I all dogs have inherited, through many generations of selection, certain patterns of behavior. In training, our best results may be obtained by building on this fact.

Every dog has reflexes. He hears a sound, and cocks his ears; he smells food, his mouth waters; he tastes disagreeable food, and spits it out; he touches a hot coal, and jerks his foot away, and so on *ad infinitum.* We can let him be a child of nature and do whatever his reflexes cause him to do, or we can condition his reflexes so that he does what we want him to do. Most dogs are practically untrained because the owners are too ignorant, too indolent— or both—to train them.

This is the way a reflex is conditioned: simultaneously with the stimulus which evokes the action we add another stimulus—a sound, a flash of light, or a sensation. If the two occur enough times together, either part of the combination may be dispensed with and the dog will react in the same uniform way. Salivation was the original reaction on which conditioning was studied,

The use of a tiny reward is employed to teach the dog to sit up. Repetition of the command is necessary before he learns to sit up without having the reward held over his nose.

and it makes as good a one as any to use as an illustration. Show a dog food and his mouth waters. Ring a bell at the same time you show him food, and his mouth waters. Repeat many times. Now ring the bell without the food being present, and his mouth will water just the same.

How does this differ from such an action as the following? You are walking around the rough in a golf course. Your dog has been taught to retrieve golf balls—an uncommonly easy feat for him. You throw a golf ball into the rough and he retrieves it by sight and by its odor. He learns by the direction you swing your arm where to run. So now you swing your arm but do not throw a ball. Away he tears into the rough and sniffs around for the rubbery odor. He finds a faint odor and gets a golf ball, bringing it to you. With a dog equipped with such a conditioned reflex you can earn spending money and get exercise most enjoyably.

Or another—your puppy scratches at the lower corner of the door to get outside. You see him doing it and open the door for him. He repeats this a few times and has thereby become conditioned to "know how to get out." And by the same token, to get in.

Or how does the saliva illustration differ from the case where your dog jumps up against you. This you have inadvertently conditioned him to do previously. But now you decide that it must stop, so you seem to pet him as you have always done, but as you cover his eyes with a hand you also step on a

Dogs of all ages appreciate toys, which they come to regard as companions.

hind foot, hard enough to hurt him. You and every other member of the family step on his foot every time he jumps up, but you try not to let your dog know you do it. What have you accomplished? You have simply made him realize that jumping up gives him a pain in a hind foot. So he doesn't jump up.

If you have never thought about it, remember that you must give a meaning to a sound. Words are sounds of no meaning to your dog until you have impressed on him what the meaning of each word is. A toot on a whistle, the ringing of a bell, the sound of a hunter's horn, and even the hum of the motor in a certain car are all sounds which can be given meanings. Giving meaning to sounds is a principal part of training.

Ideal training conditions as many reflexes at one time as possible. Actually much more of a dog's brain is involved in the conditioning of most reflexes than was formerly thought. When a dog feels a hot coal, not only does his foot snap away from it, his whole body recoils, and he trots a considerable distance from the pain-producing spot.

Conditioning over and over amounts to habit formation. That you must keep in mind. Results may be achieved by punishments and by rewards. Punishments may be the sort of thing which the dog realizes he brings on himself, such as an electric shock when he barks, or he may have an out-and-out realization that his misdeed causes you to punish him.

Rewards may be accomplishments—the realization that an action brought the desired result—or they may simply be some food you give the dog when he is hungry. Rewards supply your dog with fulfillment of a strong desire. As an example, you take his kennel mates for a walk and leave him behind. He jumps frantically at the gate and strikes the latch. The door opens: he dashes after you. Two or three repetitions of this behavior, and the dog has learned how to open the door. Or he is hungry, and he learns that doing a certain act a certain way brings a reward—food.

To train, we need to establish in our dog a great want—a drive, a stimulus—which we can fulfill with a reward, and to keep on supplying the reward until we have carried our conditioning forward to such an extent that it becomes the established pattern of behavior.

These rewards psychologists call reinforcements. Now what are some of the drives and the rewards which you can use in training?

Food. Small tidbits to be given only when the dog is *hungry*.

Companionship. Used negatively—making a dog think you are leaving home when he wants to go can have excellent results.

Love of work. Giving your dog an opportunity to do what his inherited behavior patterns urge him to do can be an excellent reward. Suppose he loves to hunt rabbits, and at every opportunity will go out into a brush lot and drive rabbits by the hour; simply giving him this privilege can be used as a reward. Letting him retrieve is an excellent illustration. He naturally, by inheritance, loves to carry small objects. He also naturally loves to run after one, but he doesn't know you will throw it until you have shown him. So in a few minutes he will learn that to drop the object at your feet means that you will throw it and that is all the reward he needs. You need not give him food for returning the object, but if you do, you will reinforce the lesson even more strongly.

Brushing with a stiff brush can act as a reward once a dog has been taught to stand. You can show him the brush and point to a chair or table, and he will bounce on to it. Or you can say a word—chair, table—and he will act the same way after a few lessons.

On the negative side, what means of punishment are available for training? First, the old, simple methods:

The open hand. A sharp slap beside the face is generally an excellent punishment. Don't let anyone convince you that the hand must be used only to reward the dog. The hand, he soon learns is just, rewarding for right acts, and disciplining for wrong.

The feet. Many experienced dog trainers believe that a dog watches their feet first, so they use them as indicators and as means of punishment. Big-game hunters often ride down miscreant hounds who have run on deer tracks and let the horse trample them. Some dog trainers kick and stamp on their dogs or, as some Midwestern backwoodsmen say, tromp on 'em, and whether we approve or not, they have dogs that work for them like demons, and behave ideally.

The rolled newspaper. This makes a crackling noise when the dog is struck with it. The trouble is that most amateur dog trainers do not strike hard enough.

Shaking. There are few more satisfactory means of punishing than picking the misbehaving dog up by the neck and shaking him until you think his teeth will drop out. A mild shake at first, of course, but violent if the mild one has proved ineffective.

The switch. A proper switching must really hurt the dog. Don't "cut the tail off an inch at a time" by a lot of annoying little taps, but pick the miscreant up by the back of the neck and wallop him along the side.

The broom. There is no more natural means of punishment in the hands of a woman than a broom. A good swish is excellent punishment for a puppy, and for a really obstreperous dog, a well-worn broom makes a wonderful tool. But it must never be used to chase a dog with. The dog must be tied where he can't crawl into a doghouse or under a bed. A barking dog can be chained to a radiator, for instance, and when he barks, the words *be quiet* can be said accompanied by a wallop with the broom. After a while you can discontinue using the broom and *be quiet* is all you need say.

The dark closet. Most dogs dread being alone and confined in the dark. For punishment, simply bundling the dog ignominiously into a dark closet for an hour can be used to excellent effect.

Water. Squirting water on an outdoor dog, throwing a half bucket of cold water over him, and filling the bucket and leaving it where he can see it ready for the next lesson works well. So does placing a half barrel of water next to his kennel and, when he barks, rushing out, making him realize he is calling you, and picking him up and pushing him under the water. But water is a warm weather punishment of course.

The electric shocker. For many years now—more than thirty—I have occasionally used a device I made which beats every other method of negative training. This is based on a dog's dislike of an electric shock. An amount of electricity which to us is almost pleasant will make a dog recoil with a jolt. And if such punishment is properly used there is no better method. I like it because it makes the dog realize that his action gives him a shock. Anyone can make such a device, but only a serious trainer or breeder is likely to do so. It consists of a dry cell, a small induction coil, a dog collar with pointed studs (two on each side, with two insulated), and a pair of wires running from the studs to the coil. There is a switch, of course. The collar is placed on the dog and the double wire acts as a leash. To give you one example of its use if the dog chews on his leash a touch of the switch gives him a shock and one or two shocks will stop such an action.

There are a few specifications of punishments which must be kept in mind:

It should hurt or frighten him. This is nature's way. Watch dogs discipline one another, or a bitch teaching her pups, and you realize that anything you or I are likely to do will be mild by comparison.

It must make your dog know that you are his boss and master, and no fooling.

You must not undertaken any training on even a small problem unless you are prepared to follow through to final conditioning.

In positive conditioning there should be no punishment until your dog is performing the act correctly at least 75 per cent of the time. That is the punishment must be for the dog failing to do something he has learned and knows how to do.

Punishment must be immediate, if possible as part of the wrong act of the dog, like the burn from the hot coal, or the electric shock or mouth burn when a puppy chews an electric cord. A dog's attention may be on something entirely different, if punishment is postponed, and you will give him the feeling he is being punished for that instead of the act for which you are really chastising him. A good illustration of such stupid training is when a dog owner returns home and finds a dog has evacuated indoors and he sticks the dog's nose in the stool and scolds. I doubt that any dog who ever lived was housebroken by that method.

TRAINING THE HOUSE DOG

Behavior training classes have become exceedingly popular, but not nearly so popular as they should be. Behavior training is basically the training of a dog to be a good companion. But it goes much further than that, because those who are bitten by this benign bug become filled with enthusiasm and the spirit of competition, and show no desire to quit. Soon they are exhibiting their dogs for prizes, and many people go on from one class to another, often aiding the newcomers to learn the lessons they have already learned themselves.

Almost all of the trainers were taught in the old or force system: that is, you push your dog's rear end down and say *sit* until he has learned to do it to order. Contrast this system's result with those of the reward system of getting the dog to sit of his own volition and then rewarding him! Surely the latter is ten times as efficient.

POSITIVE TRAINING

Let us take a few simple positive acts we wish our dog to perform. What shall our incentive or drive be? Hunger. That is painless and, apparently, magic. So we shall see our pet has only water to drink for 36 hours. He will then be hungry enough really to *try*. (He will not be harmed—a dog has lived for 117 days on water without food.)

We are going to teach him:

1. To get on the *table*. This is a useful command for him to execute,

A neat gate is easily made to restrict the dog to the use of one room.

because an old table makes an excellent place on which to comb and brush him;

2. *Down* from the table;
3. *Shake hands;*
4. *Other paw;*
5. *Lie down;*
6. *Stand;*
7. *Sit.*

How long would it take by the force method to train him to execute these seven commands? Try it on your dogs if you have untrained ones, and compare. By the reward method you will certainly have your dog executing the orders within two evenings if you keep him hungry. Starve him first for 36 hours, after which your reward will be his food. Then give him nothing but water again for 24 hours. Then let him rest a day, and thereafter feed him only what he barely needs to live on. He should be hungry enough to eat eagerly a dry crust of bread, and you will choose something more tempting than that. I suggest half-inch lumps of frankfurter or pieces of hamburger as large as a thimble.

You have probably read enough about training, or seen enough of it, to know that nearly all trainers want you to pronounce your dog's name before any command. But this I know is entirely unnecessary unless you are training a lot of dogs performing together and want to call one out from the pack to perform individually. "George—sit" and "George—lie down" and "George —jump" get tiresome and are needless. Your dog knows you are talking to him.

Get on the *table*. Your key word is *table*. So use only that. Set a chair beside your training table; neither of them must shake or tremble. With Nero—that's your dog's name in this chapter—having sniffed the reward in your hand, you say *table* and let him follow your hand first up on the chair and thence on to the table. He gets his reward and wants more.

Down from the table. Say *down*, and let him follow your hand down. When he is down, he gets his reward.

Pause a minute, get his attention, and say *table*, going through the same routine as many times as it takes for him to get on the table without a movement of your hand. All this will probably take you 30 minutes at most.

Shake hands. Put a harness or collar on Nero. Put a ring—an eye bolt—in the wall behind the table, which will be tight against the wall. The ring should be about ten inches from the table top. Run a light chain with a swivel in it from the ring in the harness or collar back to the ring in the wall. This chain should be just long enough for Nero's chest to come even with the front edge of the table.

Did you ever see what a hungry dog does when he can't reach food with his mouth? He reaches for it with his paw, doesn't he? Take advantage of that fact. Let Nero smell the meat, and the moment his foot comes forward to reach it, say *shake*, and give him his reward. In a few minutes you'll have him batting at you when you say *shake*. Then it is your time to teach him *other*.

Other paw. When he finds pawing with one foot doesn't get him the food, he will try to reach it with the other foot which will be accompanied by your word *other*. Feed him only for the correct foot coming forward on the word *other*. He will soon learn that *shake* means the right foot and *other* the left, or, if you prefer, *shake* may mean whichever he presents first and *other* the alternate foot.

After he is proficient at this job on the table, let him get down and try his reactions on the floor.

The second evening can well start with repetition of the previous evening's training before beginning new commands.

Lie down. Tie Nero with a short chain running from his harness or collar to the ring in the wall behind him. Let him shake a few times and then say *lie down*, and hold your reward just below the table top so he must lie down to reach it. When he is down, give it to him.

Stand. At once teach him what *stand* means. I like the word *up* but, as you will see, the word *hup* is used as a field trial command meaning to sit, and the two words sound too much alike for contradictory uses.

In the case of a sensitive dog, a severe scolding may be all that's necessary to train him from getting on the furniture.

You teach *stand* by holding the reward high so that Nero has to stand up to get it.

Sit is taught by holding the reward in your closed hand close to his face and making him back up. He will soon sit, and you say the word as he does so. Repeat until he knows the meaning of the word.

Having taught him this simple execution of your words, or, to put it another way, having conditioned Nero to associate word sounds with actions, you can go on applying the principle to actions off the table.

Repetition over and over again finally evokes immediate response to the words. If he does not respond, he needs more table training. Here are a few useful actions you can elicit by the use of words:

Come. Train your hungry Nero in an enclosure. Let him wander away and say *come* or just whistle. Feed him his little reward and wait for him to wander again. When you and he have repeated the action so many times that he seems to understand the word, try him another day in the open with a long training cord. When he seems to respond without a mistake, get a friend to provide something alluring, to see if the dog will fail to mind you. Walking a strange dog on a leash where Nero can see him is one of the best lures. Hold on to the training cord so the dog completely upsets himself when he comes to its end, and when he is thus discommoded call him and reward him when he comes. Or let a cat out of a bag so he can see it run away. Call *come*, and when he fails to do it, he tumbles in a heap at the end of a training cord. A few such lessons teach him that you can reach out and control him. You can then make the cord longer and longer.

Please note that you cannot train Nero vicariously: you do it, not sit in an armchair and think about it.

Fetch or *get* is a useful action to teach, and easier than many know. Since Nero loves to retrieve, just throw anything and he will run to it, pick it up, and carry it. If you start with a hungry Nero, you can use reward to teach him to discriminate between several objects, say a brush, a slipper, and his leash. Under negative training we shall see how to train a dog to realize what *no* means. In this case you can throw two objects and tell Nero to *get slipper*. If he starts to pick up the brush which you have tossed with the slipper you say *no*, and then when he picks up the slipper and brings it to you, he gets his reward. Later you can teach him what *brush* means, and *leash*, so you can throw out all three objects and he will retrieve the one you tell him to bring you.

From his differentiating in this way it is only a step to teach him to get your slippers, his brush, or his leash whenever you request them, or to take the evening paper from the paper boy and bring it to you.

I hope that by now you see how easy it is to train. Of course it takes hours of patient repetition as you give word and other sound meanings to Nero, but what could be more worth-while?

Teaching him to walk at your side, which obedience class trainers call *heeling* is only a matter of walking with Nero, keeping him on a leash at your left side, and commanding him to *sit* every time you stop. I prefer the words *at side* for this, and to train him that *heel* means what it used to; namely, to walk behind me just as the heel-driving Shepherd dogs "dog the footsteps" of cattle, sheep or their owners, or Dalmatians heel behind horses. All one needs is a leash and a switch and some reward to accomplish both objectives.

NEGATIVE TRAINING

This general kind of training in what not to do is simpler and requires much less thought than positive training, and here is where punishments are used intelligently.

When a dog misbehaves, he is not doing it because he is necessarily innately bad or trying to annoy you: he was inadvertently trained that way by you or someone previously. The barking dog furnishes an excellent example. It is a natural reaction for any dog to bark. He begins very young, and usually nothing is done to stop him. Why wouldn't he bark?

As he grows older he may bark when he is hungry. What does his owner, who is annoyed by the barking do? Unfortunately he feeds him, and thus reinforces the barking reaction to hunger.

Once a reflex has become conditioned in this way, to uncondition it is to see

The White Standard, Dorleen's Mystic Moselle, U. D., Eileen P. Larkin, North Kingston, Rhode Island, owner. Retrieving his dumbell and taking the hurdle in beautiful fashion.

either that it is not used for several months, or to shock the dog severely with punishment, so that the one reaction overcomes the other. We know this not only from animal psychology, but from human. Most of us have been conditioned in certain ways: to stand when "The Star Spangled Banner" is played, for example, and if we were to sit when it was played before a ball game we should have a guilty feeling. For months after Hitler died, if someone said "Heil, Hitler" to a German, it was difficult for the hearer not to salute.

It took a lot of training to condition these dogs for such a performance. They are Charborn Camee of Puttencove, Betty Van Sciver, Malvern, Pennsylvania, owner and Ma Folie Meredith, C. D. X., Mrs. Carl Necker, Philadelphia, Pennsylvania, owners.

The less-complicated dog acts simply, positively, and negatively. So, brainwashing for him—washing out the previously conditioned reflexes—can best be achieved by punishment. We have seen what some of those methods can be. And now, knowing roughly what the conditions are, one realizes how much sternness, persistence, and patience may be necessary to brain-wash, to decondition, and to recondition Nero. Here are a few useful negative commands and how to apply them:

No. I start every dog I ever train by teaching this simply taught expletive. It is easy to say, and the dog learns it as easily as a puppy learns to keep away from his mother's food when she growls—her way of saying *no*. And your punishment need not be so severe as the bitch's, either, to accomplish similar understanding by the puppy or dog.

If you are using your hand to discipline, drop a bone with meat on it before your hungry dog. Be sure the food is too large for him to swallow. Say *no* sharply as he goes to take it, and slap his face. Train him in an empty room where he can't hide away. I would not use an electric shocker here, because it will be ever so much more difficult to get him to take the food when you come to teach that.

As you slap him, he drops the meat. Leave it there, and every time he starts to take it say *no* and slap. In a few minutes he will know the meaning of *no* as it applies to that one object. So now you must train him to know the meaning of the sound *take it*, or *take*. You may actually have to put the meat in his mouth and let him chew on it. Keep dropping rewards and say *take it* over and over, and suddenly intersperse the *take it* with *no*. If he takes the meat, reach right into his mouth and pull it out, and slap.

When he has learned these commands, try throwing the enticing food a distance of, say, five feet from you and saying *no*. and, once the dog has obeyed, *take it*. Next, stand in the doorway of the room and repeat this. The whole thing should not take you more than an hour to teach Nero. Now you are ready to apply the word *no* to other activities, and if you are firm, never letting an exception occur, you will have done your dog and yourself a great service. You can use the word for anything he should not do—chase cars, bark, hook his chin on to the food or water dish and tip it, and so forth.

Stay. Staying in one spot while you, the dog's master, walk away is a negative response. Nero's natural response will be to follow you. Have him lie down, and say *stay* while you back away. If he moves say *no*. After a few minutes' delay, tell him to come, and reward him. Repeat, lengthening the delay until he will stay as long as you wish. You can accompany your command with a motion if you wish, such as a Hitler salute (this is the usual obedience-class gesture), and when you drop your hand, call *come*. Soon the dog will watch your hand, and you can dispense with the word. Practice him often, and he will become adept.

XII
Pens and Bedding

We have already discussed bedding material for little puppies as well as whelping and nest boxes. Here we take up the matter of pens and bedding for older pups. It is one of the more important questions in cynidiatrics.

If we are not fortunate enough to be able to use wire bottom pens, which will be discussed later, then we must keep puppies on something solid, and inside some house where they will be protected from the rain, the sun's direct rays, heat and cold. Until I invented the wire bottom pen for puppies, mine were regularly raised on the ground, in winter and in summer. This brings us to a consideration of how much cold a little puppy can stand, provided of course, he is with his mother. The answer seems to be that he can stand very low temperatures so long as he is dry and has his mother to cuddle against, and something under him which he can heat. I never can recall losing one from cold. Over the front of the doors of their houses was hung a few thicknesses of burlap. Under them was six inches of packed straw. Usually they were whelped in these houses. Each house had a porch. If a bitch whelped on a very cold night, she was taken inside so that the puppies would not be frozen when they were wet. The bitches were always taken inside to whelp so someone could sit with them, when there was some reason for wanting to save as many puppies as possible. The puppies were generally put outside again the day after they were born. No harm resulted.

Think of these puppies raised in the cold of the north. Yes, they can stand a lot of cold so long as they have their mother with them. But let her desert them and they soon freeze. Indeed they seem to stand cold much better than heat. They can reduce their temperatures to some extent by panting, but to no such extent as they can when grown. I have seen fewer puppies recover from overheating than from chilling.

So, houses for puppies should be sufficiently solid to keep out winds in the winter and sufficiently ventilated to allow for cooling in the summer. If the box is large enough for the mother to stand in after the bedding is packed down, and six inches longer and wider than she is long, it will be large enough.

Bedding can be almost any absorbent material which has good insulating qualities. Some breeders have done well with bare boards in the summertime when puppies were housebroken, but in winter time and summer too, when there is mud present, bedding is generally advisable. Straw, hay, sugar cane

Too young to be clipped, but not too young to appreciate a comfortable bed.

and shavings all are good. Change the bedding every 7 days at the outside so that worm eggs will not have a chance to incubate and no worm damage can result.

MATERIAL FOR RUNS

One of the first things that occurs to puppy raisers is that they should obtain the cleanliness of concrete runs. Now, actually there are probably few worse media on which to raise dogs than concrete. If the surface is made glass smooth as, it must be to be sanitary, it becomes very slippery in wet weather. When it is coarse, the surface sometimes will harbor millions of worm eggs. To keep it clean requires constant scrubbing with a stiff brush and much water. The wormiest puppies that are brought to our hospital are those raised on concrete.

The hoe or shovel used to take up the stools just scrapes over the surface, usually painting it with stool, filling up the roughness and affording the most admirable environment for the worm eggs to incubate in. Admirable, that is, from the point of view of the parasite, but filthy from the point of view of the dog. Many people have had their concrete runs chopped out because of their difficulty in raising clean puppies on them.

Another material not to use is gravel. It sounds very fine to say "My puppies have fine feet; no wonder, they are raised in packed gravel runs." But that gravel offers a very coarse surface and cleaning stools from it is next to impossible.

The same may be said for cinders.

The best material that we have ever found is washed sand. It is inexpensive and clean, easy to renew, easy to remove stools from, without rough surfaces in which part of each stool can hide. As each stool is removed a little sand may be scraped up with it. As the pens are cleaned the sand is gradually removed and soon needs replenishing. Several times a year the whole surface for two inches may be dug off and renewed at small cost. The runs seldom have any odor. The sand soon packs solidly and its appearance is good.

It, like all others except concrete runs, offers the objection of affording a wonderful place for the dogs to dig in. The surface is sometimes irregular due to the propensity to dig, especially in summertime. Some breeders have gotten around this by pouring concrete runs four inches lower than the final surface of the runs and covering them with sand. This does away with the digging but prevents drainage, with the result that the sand stays wet too long after a rain.

Grass runs look very nice. Portable pens are often advertised which may be moved all over a lawn. How excellent this seems to the amateur! But the appeal is quickly lost after trial. The spot becomes covered with stool—and puppies' stools are often soft—and nobody wants to lie on the spot where the pen was placed for many a day. If there are fleas on the puppies, the eggs develop in the lawn, and all in all, the whole practice has so little to recommend it that only one who had never tried it would succumb to the enticements of the beautiful advertisements we see to sell such pens. Even if we could be sure that the puppies' stools were extra firm, and we took them up as fast as they were deposited, the lawn is still no fit place to raise a pup.

WIRE BOTTOM PENS

The first public suggestion on the value of wire bottomed pens for rearing little puppies came from the author in an article in Popular Science, entitled "Wire Walking Puppies". The second was a popular article in the American Kennel Gazette. Both of these articles told of the value of such pens in the raising of puppies, not only in their early life but up until they were grown.

Since that time, thousands of these cages have been built and found to keep dogs as well as puppies in excellent condition. Wire bottoms are being used in pet shops, under sick dogs in hospitals, and in many and sundry ways where it is desirable to keep dogs out of their own or other dogs' filfth.

Today we can give the experiences of nineteen years in raising puppies on wire. Literally thousands of puppies have been raised in this manner. Every puppy attests to the fact that the method is not harmful, but very beneficial. It is good for the professional and is even better for the individual who has no kennel and who is planning to raise a single litter of puppies in his home or apartment.

The whole progress of the wire bottom pen has been one of great caution. For many years people raised pet squirrels on it. Then the mink breeders and

A practical type of bed, much better than wood or wicker because the dog can't disfigure it by chewing on it.

raccoon breeders began using it. The fox men tried it also. We dog breeders were the last, and many who tried it, often in the first experiments with them, did so in such a gingerly fashion that sometimes it was almost comical.

What held nearly everyone back was the wonder whether the wire was going to harm the puppies' feet. I was no exception. But after just one try I plunged and wouldn't exchange the system for any other, at least none that I have seen. Thousands of these wire bottom pens have been built and are being used all over America.

My work calls me to homes where many litters of puppies have been raised. Usually the pups are in the cellar. Sometimes, one doesn't need to be told that there are puppies in the cellar, because on being admitted through the front door, one's nose tells all. Anyone who has tried to raise puppies in the cellar knows what they do to the floor. It is almost impossible to keep such a cellar clean. Spread newspapers around all you will, take them up as often as you want, but there is still plenty of odor left in the floor. Very few people realize how rough is the surface of a concrete floor. A hoe can be scraped over it and there is still much stool left in the pores or valleys, speaking microscopically. And because of this it is very difficult to eliminate the worms from infected puppies. They may be cleaned out of the intestines, but if there are worm eggs in the bottoms of the concrete pores, the puppies will continue to pick them up. If you looked at a worm egg with a microscope

Some Poodles are benched in individual cages and some are chained to the flat boards.

and saw it at the bottom of a tiny depression in the concrete, it might be, relatively speaking, about as large as a tennis ball on the floor of the room, if the ceiling of the room represented the surface of the concrete. No amount of scrubbing or sweeping will disinfect the cellar; it may help to deodorize it. Remember, too that a heated cellar is an excellent environment to incubate worm eggs, or for hookworm larvae and fleas to develop.

So, if you are going to raise puppies in your cellar or any other part of your house, put them on wire so that the feces will have to drop on newspaper which won't move, because the puppies' feet never touch it. That paper may be rolled up and burned and fresh paper put down, and a much cleaner litter result. A much sweeter smelling home will also result.

Probably no better way has yet been devised for inside rearing of puppies in winter than raising them on wire, at least until the puppies are half grown. Allowing them to have daily runs is worthwhile to develop muscles. But this is not necessary. We have never seen poor muscular development result from raising puppies to maturity in this fashion. Repeatedly I have raised litters of small sized dogs from birth to maturity in food tests, and in other studies, with only good results. The lack of exercise does not cause muscular shrinking. If greater muscles are desired, exercise at maturity is sufficient.

I realize that there will be those who will say it is cruel to keep puppies in this way. But that is not so. If they never know any other existence, they will not miss what they don't know. Sometimes the very people who have told me it was cruel were those who sat in a rocking chair more than half their lives and actually took perhaps a tenth as much exercise as a litter of puppies get in a wire bottom pen. They play and frisk and have a fine time. No, it is not cruel.

CONSTRUCTION OF WIRE BOTTOM PENS

The wire part of the pen illustrated is 3 ft. by 6 ft. This will accommodate six small puppies of any breed or four grown cocker spaniels. The pen is 2 ft. high and stands 1 ft. off the ground, bringing the tops of the cages to about the same height as an ordinary table.

The top of the hutch folds back over the wire top, permitting puppies to be stood there and displayed or groomed.

In the cage part is a door, 1 ft. by 3 ft. which opens back, as may be seen in the drawing.

The hutch is 2 ft. by 3 ft. This is plenty large enough to be used as whelping quarters for dogs weighing up to 30 lbs. Larger pens are naturally required for the larger breeds. The illustration shows a battery of wire bottom pens used in one of the veterinary colleges. These have been constructed somewhat differently. The extra leg is located at the back of the hutch, which is a good idea. If it is placed at the front of the hutch, when a lot of heavy puppies

A battery of wire-bottomed cages. Raised in such cages dogs have excellent feet and the parasite problem is kept to a minimum. They are of more interest to the kennel owner than to the owner of one dog.

Part of the Poodle section of a dog show. The cages are used not to prevent the dogs from biting passers by, but rather for their own protection and comfort.

fill the hutch, there is a possibility of the cage's tipping backward unless another leg is also placed under the back.

In constructing the pens, it is advisable to staple the wire onto the inside of the 2 × 3 in. framework so as to allow no rim on which feces can collect. Then the heavy 1 in. mesh wire on the bottom can be stapled on last. This wire must be strong, and the staples should be longer than ordinary poultry wire staples.

Wire for the top and sides is 1 × 2 in. turkey, heavy gauge, such as is sold for fox ranches, and should be tightly stretched. It is almost essential to run a brace across the middle of the bottom stringers to which the square mesh wire can be stapled. You can have a blacksmith bend a light piece of angle iron the ends at right angles and bore holes through the ends so that the brace may be attached to the inside of the stringers, thus preventing the wire from sagging. If this brace is not used, sags develop that in time lead to breaks, which necessitate attaching new wire.

Remember, it does not pay to skimp by buying lightweight wire. The heavier grades have proven themselves to be much more economical over a period of time.

The suggestions above are given as a starting basis. They have been found to be practical and economical, but you may have ideas of your own that will work out much better in your particular circumstances. You can exercise your ingenuity in developing variations which answer your individual requirements.

XIII
Exercising and Grooming

The plain truth is that no puppy needs more exercise than he gets in a pen six by ten feet in dimension. It is nice to give him more—his leg muscles will be better developed—but it is not essential to exercise him. The best part of it is that taking him for a walk exercises you.

Many people when they say "exercise a dog" mean taking him for a walk where he can evacuate and urinate. If you had seen as many thousands of happy puppies of all sizes—even Saint Bernards—grow to full size in runs eight by twenty feet, you would realize how little exercise puppies need. Hundreds of beagles and cocker spaniels have been raised in wire-bottom runs three by six feet, and because they never know anything else, they have been supremely happy.

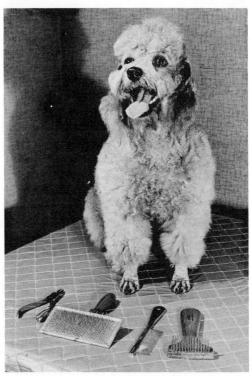

Useful Grooming Tools:
Wire Brush for smoothing the outside of the coat; *Steel Comb*, the most useful implement for Poodle grooming; *A Rake* to remove loose hair and to unsnarl knots in the coat.

The rake is useful as a first step in combing out the ears after which the comb produces the fringe effect.

But we said *need*, not *how much puppies can stand*. Five-month old puppies, which were raised in eight-by-twenty foot pens have been taken for six-mile walks the first time they ever left their pens and one is amazed at their endurance. But then, few persons realize how much a mature dog can stand. Sled dogs, six to a team pull sleds with ton loads miles and miles a day. Foxhounds have been known to run forty-eight hours pursuing foxes, and during that time may run well over three hundred miles.

So exercise, while not necessary, is most pleasant. And there are simple, useful ways to exercise your puppy. If he is a hunter, get him into the woods and fields to accustom him to the environment he will come to love. If he is a retriever, teach him to fetch. Go to an open place and throw a ball. Fifty yards is a short retrieve. While you stand in one place, the pup runs one hundred yards for each throw. Seventeen retrieves and he has run a mile.

If you live near a golf links, teach your pup to retrieve a golf ball.

Puppies of larger breeds can be taught to pull wagons or sleds by the time

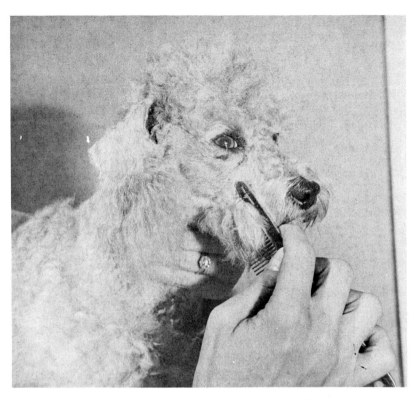

Here the groomer uses a comb in combing out the whiskers.

they are six months old. Some puppies love to swim and will bring out sticks the owner throws into the water. If you have no natural way to exercise your pup, don't worry; he'll probably be just about as healthy with none.

Probably rough playing gives puppies all the exercise they need. Some puppies will play with you, some with toys which they will toss into the air, wrestle with, then chew on. Give your pup plenty of playtime and encourage playing up to the point where he bites too sharply. Old rag dolls make excellent playthings. Even a well-knotted towel amuses some pups for hours. If you give him a rubber toy, be sure he doesn't chew it apart and swallow the pieces. During teething, pups love to chew, and chewing becomes almost play with them. Encourage it throughout teething—from three and half to six months of age—but stop it if the puppy uses his second teeth where he shouldn't.

COMBING AND BRUSHING

It is well to realize that by properly combing and brushing your pup you

193

"Danbe's Pepe La Moke", a standard White Poodle shown in Puppy clip. Photo by Louise Van der Meid with the cooperation of the Noonan's of Long Beach, Calif.

Evelyn Miller and her Silver Miniature, Gigi. Gigi was bred in England by Mr. and Mrs. Norman Elliott of Southampton. Checking your Poodles teeth regularly is highly recommended as many times as a cleaning is in order.

The wire brush is the last grooming implement to be used. It is useful only for surface grooming.

can do a lot toward his training. When puppies are small and easily controlled, you can teach them that grooming tools won't hurt them; even get them to enjoy being groomed. Watch a dog at a dog show being groomed. He will stand like a statue while the handler goes over him.

Set your puppy on a table at arm's length. Never hug him while you work on him. After a while you can stand back and view him from all sides, while the pup stands because he enjoys it. Use a strong comb with teeth of the proper spacing. Professionals generally use one with twelve teeth to the inch, and teeth one inch long. Push the teeth right down to the skin and comb until no knots remain. You can pull them out quite easily from puppy coats, or if they are too tenuous, cut them lengthwise with scissors and then comb. If your pup brings in twigs, leaves, and in general gets easily snarled you must comb often. But by all means be the boss and if the puppy objects, don't stop combing. Many a pup has learned that he can bluff his owner by objecting to a combing and in this way is easily trained to become a vicious dog. If, however, he does object, place a tie about his face and finish the job once you start it.

Sometimes a puppy may need to be held in place by a cord from above attached to his collar. It is usually possible to arrange such a cord, which can be shortened as he grows. This can be done by putting a table in a doorway. Affix a hook to the top of the doorway and drop a cord from it to the puppy's collar.

CLIPPING

If your pup needs trimming, accustom him to stand on a table like a show dog where he will be independent. The person who clips for you will appreciate this early training.

Puppies are ordinarily clipped on the face and feet by the time they are four or five months old, and some even younger, at six and eight weeks.

NAIL CARE

If only to save nylons or prevent runs in sweaters and so forth, a puppy's nails should be kept trimmed. But there are other reasons, most important of which is the effect long nails have on a pup's feet. If the nails are allowed to grow too long, the toes will become tipped upward, which in turn will cause some pain and also a foot which does not develop naturally. Persons buying puppies appreciate it greatly if the nails are cut before the pups leave the kennel.

Only the tips of the nails are trimmed. When the dog stands, the nail tips should barely touch the ground.

Daniel and Bette Noonan own "Jaynel Danbe's Lisette", a 9 month old Cream White Female puppy in English Saddle clip. Photo by Louise Brown Van der Meid.

Gigi, belonging to Evelyn Miller, though a well trained Poodle, isn't too happy about posing in a raincoat under hot photo lights.

In an ungroomed dog long nails will frequently catch in his ears when he scratches himself. Sometimes the pads of the foot actually overgrow, so that instead of a good hard surface the front of the pad will appear spongy, and this overgrowth will need to be trimmed off frequently—a practise which is never necessary if the nails are kept short.

Your veterinarian will trim them for you, or you can buy a pair of clippers and keep them trimmed at home. In young pups it is a simple matter to trim off the hook or transparent part. But as the puppy grows it is not so easy to know where the "quick" begins and where the nail will bleed. At this point there are nerves, so the puppy will let you know when you are too close.

If you have patience and time, use a nail file and keep the nails filed off. A good rule is to have the nail just long enough to touch the ground when the dog is standing. Many dog owners keep their pets' nails filed. Dogs running on concrete keep their own nails filed. Only their dewclaw nails grow too long because those nails do not reach the ground to wear off.

What if you trim the nails too closely and they bleed? No harm whatever comes of it except the damage the blood does to the floors or to your clothing. In fact, the toenails of some dogs, if they are allowed to grow too long, will nearly always bleed when they are cut off to the correct length. This applies particularly to dogs where the blood seems to come almost to the tip of the nail no matter how long it grows. The nails of such dogs should be kept filed at regular intervals.

If a veterinarian cuts your dog's nails and they bleed, you will notice that he wraps the foot in a bandage and tells you to wait until you get home to remove it. Be sure to keep the dog off concrete for a day, because this will wear the end off the nail and cause it to start bleeding again.

If you cut the nails yourself and they bleed, be sure to cover them for a while with bandage until bleeding stops.

CARE OF THE EARS

Your young puppies seldom need to have their ears cleaned.

Dirty ear canals may be brought to your attention in several ways. One way you may become aware of this condition is to have your pup shake his head and scratch at his ears a great deal of the time, or you may notice a heavy, dark, waxy discharge. Another indication is a strong odor which exudes from certain infections.

Many products are presently being used very successfully for ear-cleaning purposes. Propylene glycol is one such material.

Place the pup on a table or raised place. Take an ear flap in your left hand so that the ear canal is exposed and pour enough propylene glycol in the ear canal to almost completely fill it with fluid. Massage the base of the ear and take up the fluid which runs out of the ear with a small piece of cotton.

Propylene glycol can be obtained at any drugstore, or your veterinarian may prescribe some other medication which is equally effective for dissolving wax in the ear canal.

All Poodles grow hair in the ear canals. This hair must be kept pulled out or it becomes matted with wax and canker develops. Strangely enough, there is little pain associated with its removal. Some dogs seem to enjoy it. All you need is a pair of forceps. Pointed electrician's pincers will do if none of the surgical types are available. A great deal can be extracted with the thumb and finger because the hair loosens quite easily.

ANAL GLANDS

Every dog has a pair of glands, which are part of his skin located on either side of and just below the opening of his anus. These are called the anal glands. When the dog becomes terrified, each gland discharges its contents through a tiny tube or duct. If the dog never has a good fright, the glands may become infected and the puppy will sit down and drag himself along by his front legs—playing sleigh ride, as the children call it. If this performance fails to squeeze the contents out, an infection may produce an abscess which ruptures through the skin after first swelling greatly and causing pain.

Your veterinarian will show you how to empty the glands. If he is not near you, try it this way: Feel with your thumb and second finger to determine the location of the pair of swollen glands. They may feel like a pair of small marbles. Cover your hand with a piece of cotton. Hold the pup's tail straight up with your left hand, squeeze with your right thumb and finger, through the cotton, until you have forced all the glands' contents out through the anus onto the cotton. This material will have a most obnoxious odor. If you get any on your hand, wash it off quickly, or your hand will smell for a long while.

TEETHING AND TOOTH CARE

Look into the puppy's mouth often and watch the development of his teeth. The sharp little puppy teeth begin to shed when the pup is about fourteen weeks of age. The two upper middle incisors fall out first. It takes about two months before the new teeth are all in. You may find some of the puppy teeth around the house; he probably has swallowed the rest. No harm done.

Should your puppy have any disease during the teething period, you can expect his teeth to be pitted, due to a lack of enamel being deposited while the teeth were growing. An experienced veterinarian can look at a dog's teeth and be able to tell you which week of the pup's life he was sick. The structure of the tooth grows, but no enamel is deposited until the disease is over. And if one knows the time when the various teeth grow in, one will see how these telltale marks furnish a timetable. The discolored pits or bands remain for the puppy's life.

Evelyn Miller grooming Gigi for many of the illustrations in this book. Evelyn Miller (the wife of Dr. Herbert Axelrod), is a noted authority on dogs and has written many books on this subject.

This Brown Poodle is in need of a bit of touching up before it gets into the show ring. A miniature bitch, named "Show Me", it looks like a very promising Poodle. Brown Poodles (Chocolates and Apricots) often have brown (liver-colored) noses and toe nails. Photo by Louise Brown Van der Meid.

Fortunately, puppies' teeth seldom need cleaning, that task is reserved for later in their lives. And then chewing dog biscuits will do it.

A quite common teething trouble is the failure of the puppy canine teeth—the fangs—to fall out when the new ones come in. This may cause irritations on the lips if the first teeth are push out sideways, but usually the only harm done is that food catches between the old and new teeth. Have your puppy's doctor remove the teeth that fail to drop out.

BATHING

It seems incredible that nearly every puppy owner believes it is wrong to bathe a puppy, or let it get wet, until the pup is six months old. No one likes to advise on such a point because of the usual unscientific method of thinking which causes too many people to feel that because one event follows another, the first is the cause of the second. If I advise a client to bathe her dog and a week later the pup has pneumonia, I am to blame—I and the bath. Therefore I do not advise you. I can say I've never known of a bath in a warm house, after which the pup was dried, to produce pneumonia, and I have known of hundreds of cases of pneumonia in puppies which had not had baths, been exposed or wet. On the basis of my experience, it is much more likely that a puppy will develop pneumonia if he is not given a bath.

But, to be sensible, we all know that every puppy was born soaking wet and dried from his own body heat and that of his mother's. If one of my puppies gets dirty or smelly I bathe him, not before.

Today there are many ways of bathing puppies. You can use special dog soap, cake or liquid. Or you can use baby soaps, or household soaps, cake or

After the bath a thorough towelling is in order.

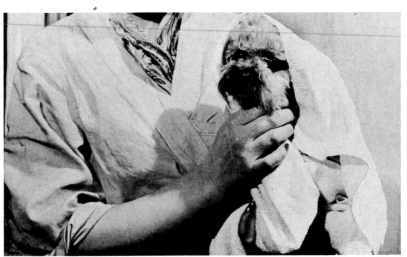

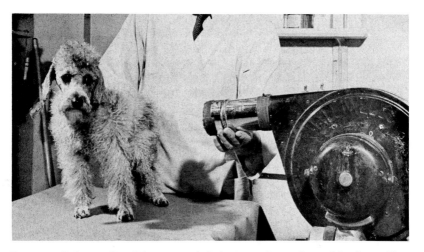

To remove the last vestige of dampness, a hair dryer gets the coat in condition for combing.

liquid. You can give him a "dry bath" by using a special preparation made in any of several ways. These are usually detergents in which bug-killing drugs are incorporated. Some leave an insecticidal residue; some do not. Some are of a dry, corn-meal powder base, some of foaming whipped-cream consistency.

Bathing is accomplished by selecting a proper place to start with. The size and condition of the puppy help to determine the place. A month-old toy puppy may be washed in a teacup, while a six-month-old large size dog needs nothing smaller than the family bathtub. If you don't mind using the tub after the dog, you can use your own. Thousands of dog owners do. Or, if you wish, you can rig up a special tub for your pet.

Some owners wash their dogs standing on the lawn, using a pail of water.

The first thing to do if you are giving a water bath is to get the soap ready. Suppose you decide on flakes. Put a handful of flakes in a pan of warm water and dissolve them. Have another pan with warm water in which is mixed some insect-killing drug, of which several are available. Put a cotton plug in each ear of the pup and he will be less inclined to shake himself. Also put on an apron of some waterproof material to protect yourself in the event the pup struggles or shakes.

The experienced dog washer realizes that water runs off his puppy's back and only slowly wets the hair and penetrates to the skin. Soap is a wetting agent. Therefore he soaps the pup as he wets him. I like to use 20% liquid soap and pour a line of it along the puppy's back. I apply water to the soap, and the mixture at once wets the whole coat. I then work up a lather by rubbing and rinse the puppy thoroughly, making sure that all the soap is washed

Two littermates . . . a Black and a Silver. Note that the outer hair on both is black, but the under hair is Silver.

Evelyn Miller's "Gigi" gave birth to three puppies (only two are shown here): a black (left) a silver (right) and a liver-pointed Chocolate.

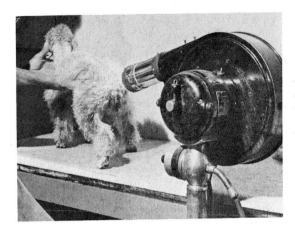

There are many kinds of hair dryers. This type is especially useful for Toys and Miniatures.

out of the coat. If there is still dirt to be seen or the odor is not gone, I soap and rinse again.

When bathing your pup, squeeze all the water you can from the pup's coat and apply the rinse. This kills any passengers and leaves a clean, fresh odor. Now rub the puppy as dry as you can with a towel and leave him where he will finish drying in a warm place.

If you prefer to give him a dry bath, follow directions on the container of whatever you buy. If a coarse powder is used, be sure to comb and brush your puppy thoroughly before you allow him his freedom. This method can clean a dog well. If you use a foaming detergent, rub it in and wipe it off thoroughly with a towel. Applying the detergent and dissolving the dirt but not removing it does no good, except to kill insects. The dirt is still on the coat, and when the pup is given his freedom he either wipes the dirt off on the rugs, furniture, or your clothes, or else it dries on him and the "bath" proves to be no bath at all.

The matter of drying is really important, especially in cold weather. Many puppy owners wash their charges in the evening, and the pups have to stay inside where it is warm to finish drying.

As puppies grow older, body odors become more pronounced. Ear canker may develop and perfume the air in the puppy's proximity with the odor of bad cheese. The pup's anal glands may become infected and he may slide along your rugs leaving an obnoxious odor. His collar or harness may accumulate the waxy secretion from his skin and acquire the typical doggy odor.

You can bathe your pup often, but such odors remain to taunt you. However, if you treat the ear canker with what your veterinarian gives you, empty the pup's anal glands occasionally, and scrape the collar, cleansing it with alcohol and then oiling it, the pup will smell sweet and clean after a bath.

XIV
Grooming Your Poodle

I have devoted an entire chapter to the grooming and care of the Poodle, because it is a very important part of Poodle owning. Clipping is something which is essential to the cleanliness and comfort of the dog. You will need to have your dog clipped anywhere from three times to six times or more during every year, depending upon the actual style of clipping that you decide you like.

Most books on grooming the Poodle start by saying how easy it is and how anyone can do it. I must disagree with these statements. Grooming the Poodle takes a great deal of skill and time. If you have perseverance and are willing to spend the amount of time it requires, you can become efficient at clipping your own Poodle.

There are certain pieces of equipment which you will need to begin your clipping chores. Here they are: Most important, of course, is a clipper. One of these can be purchased for as little as fifteen dollars or as much as fifty dollars. Naturally, the cheaper clippers are not going to provide the service which a more expensive one will, but it might be better for you to practice with a cheaper machine to determine whether this is something which you can do and want to do. Or you may want to borrow one from a friend to try it.

FINE

COARSE

These are some of the blades that Oster recommends for clipping Poodles. The finer the blade the closer the clipping. The fine blade leaves hair 1/32" long. The skip-tooth provides faster and freer feeding of long, heavy, shaggy coats.

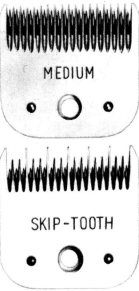

MEDIUM

SKIP-TOOTH

Poodles should be trained to stay off the furniture. A scolding should suffice ... if that doesn't work use more severe methods.

This beautiful Black Standard Poodle, owed by Mrs. Nagy, couldn't resist turning his head as the camera snapped the picture. Photo by Louise Brown Van der Meid.

Before starting to clip your dog, wash him thoroughly. Photo courtesy of Oster Co.

When you begin clipping in earnest, you will want a clipper with interchangeable heads, so that you may use blades of different sizes. The most commonly used clipper is the Oster Small Animal Clipper. The Oster Company sells blades sizes #15, #10 and #5, which will be about all the average Poodle groomer will require. I will explain later where and how these various sizes are used.

A Steel Comb should be your first implement. There are many makes to be had. A comb with teeth one inch long and twelve teeth to the inch is ideal. But many combs are made with teeth that bend under hard usage or soon drop out. In professional work we never have found the equal of the Resco comb for general use. You can obtain one at almost any dog supply store.

A brush, too, is a must, and this can be any fairly stiff and inexpensive doggie brush, or as expensive a one as you wish. Your dog will like a brushing with a stiff brush better than he will one with a soft one.

Dry your Poodle well before you begin clipping. The usual electric hair dryer, like the one illustrated, serves the purpose well. Photo courtesy of Oster Dryer.

Be sure that your Poodle is standing on a firm surface before you start clipping him.

A razor-blade dresser is useful to remove stray hair and keep the coat flat. *Scissors* are essential of course.

Toenail clippers and file. The guillotine type of the former is best. Only if you expect to show your dog will a nail file be necessary, and maybe not even then. A house dog running on concrete will file his own nails, unless you fail to keep the hair trimmed under his feet.

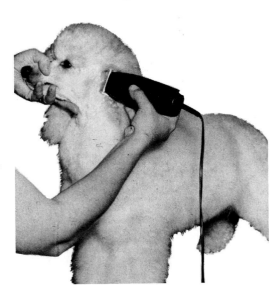

Before starting to clip your Poodle, it is wise to let him hear the sound of the clipper so that he will not be startled when you remove his hair. Photo courtesy of Oster Co.

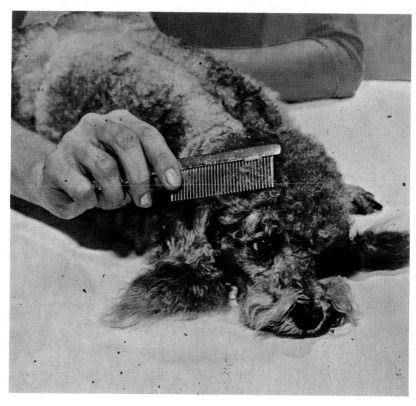

Gigi, the favorite poodle of Evelyn Miller, just loves to be combed. Thorough training instills great confidences in any Poodle.

Gigi is begging for food! The amusing part of it is that she always begs for food . . . but never eats it as she is trained not to eat anything not put into her familiar dish.

This is the proper way to grip your Poodle's face before beginning the clipping operation. It is generally conceded that the face of the Poodle is the hardest . . . and most important. Miss Miller, in the photo below, is trimming her Poodle's face prior to using the clipper. Note that she protects the moustache with her fingers!

One of the trickiest spots to clip is around the Poodle's mouth. With the the fingers of your left hand, carefully pull back the corner of the mouth to prevent cutting the dog's lip while you clip the hair from the edges. It's very important that you use extreme care to avoid nipping the skin. Courtesy of the Oster Co.

Besides these you can buy a wide variety of gadgets—thinning shears, glove brushes, oils, and so on. Get them if you wish, but with the above items an expert can put a dog into show shape.

THE ART OF GROOMING

As we have seen, it was the groomer who set the show style. Perhaps grooming really is the art it is supposed to be, but if so there are a lot of dog-clipping Rembrandts, Corots, and Rodins who learned their dog art in a week or less. I have instructed many who can turn out beautiful jobs.

If your dog is inclined to snap, tie a face tie tightly about his mouth with the knot under his chin, and, bringing the ends of your tie along the cheeks, tie them together in a bow knot behind the ears. If the dog won't stand still, move the table under a curtain pole or something to which you can attach a chain, the other end of which you fasten to the dog's collar. We assume this is his first clipping; every dog is suspicious of the buzzing clipper until he learns that it feels good on his skin.

Clipping a Poodle should be started when the puppy is fairly young. Usually anytime after three months of age is adequate to begin clipping the face, feet and base of the tail. The first couple of clippings there may be considerable objection raised by the pup, but be firm and he will eventually become accustomed to the procedure and will, after a while, seem to fall asleep while this is being done.

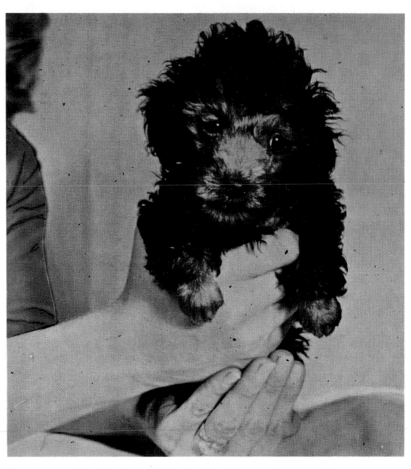

A very young Silver Miniature Poodle. Until the face and feet were trimmed it was impossible to tell this dog from a Black Poodle puppy.

Elmer and Jayne Turpin own "Minikin Slipper Silver Man", a toy silver dog, shown here in the English Saddle clip. Photo by Louise Brown Van der Meid.

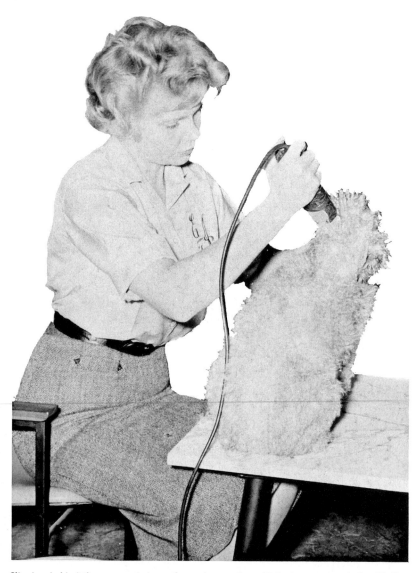

Clipping behind the ears and down the neck sometimes frightens a puppy during his first experience with the clipper. Much patience is often needed.

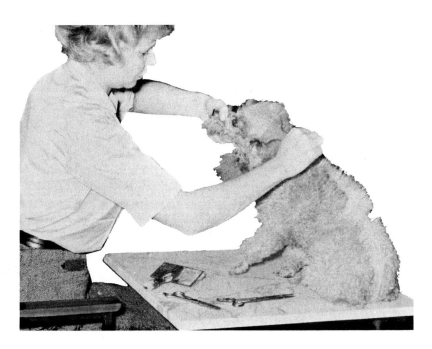

Clipping completed, the next task is to comb out the coat and use the shears for the fancy trimming about the face.

"Jaynel Danbe's Pierrette" is the name of this beautiful Apricot Toy female. Still only 3 months old, it has a lot of promise. The Poodle is wearing the Puppy clip. Photo by Louise Brown Van der Meid.

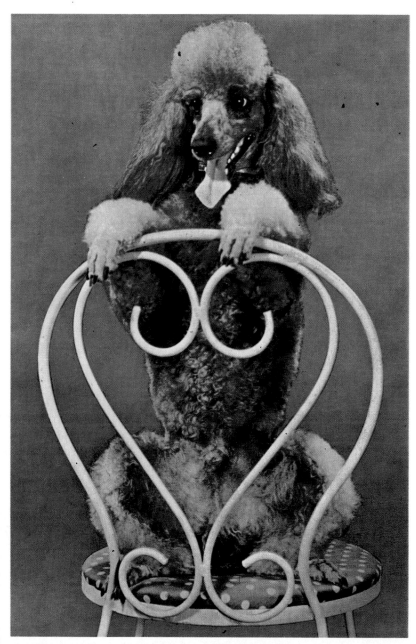

Silver Standard Poodle used for tricks. Many "professional" dogs are Poodles. Three Lions Photo.

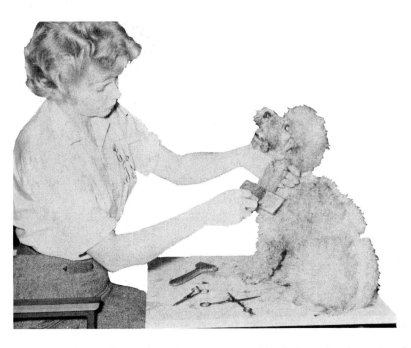

Ouch! Please pull on that comb gently. Sometimes combing feels good and sometimes it hurts, depending on how badly the hair is snarled.

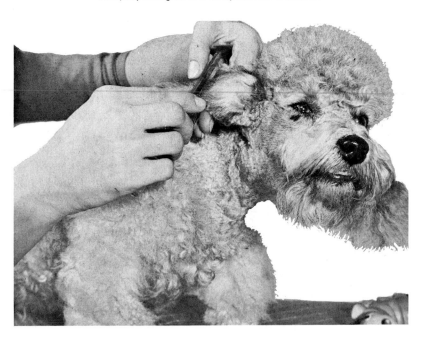

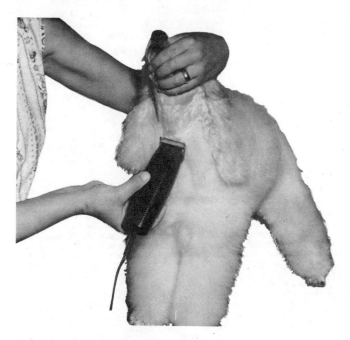

There are very few people who use the same technique of clipping the neck. In the main, the technique involved depends upon the dog and how easy he is to handle. Two techniques are shown here. Courtesy of the Oster Co.

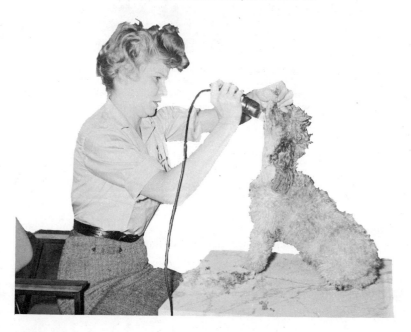

Most poodles are a bit touchy about their feet. Actually they are downright ticklish! Clip against the grain of the hair, over the arch of the toes and around the heel of the foot. Then, being very careful not to cut the web between the toes, clip the toes and hair between them to make a neat appearance. Turn the foot and clip any hair that may be growing underneath, so that it won't pick up burrs or mud.

When you have mastered this phase of your apprenticeship, you will be able to branch out and begin trying fancier and more elaborate styles of clipping.

If you plan to enter your dog in dog shows, you will not have much choice about the style of clipping. He will have to be shown in one of three styles: The Continental clip, the English Saddle clip, or the puppy clip. I will explain more fully about the clips later. But, if you do not plan to enter your dog in dog shows, then there is no limit to the large variety of ways in which you may clip him.

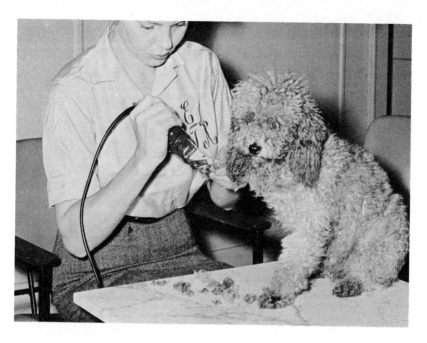

A puppy's feet are clipped gently and then trimmed with a scissors. He soon comes to learn that it doesn't hurt.

When trimming the back feet it is easier to work with the dog's back to you. Courtesy of Oster Co. Below: Evelyn Miller, noted dog authority and author of many dog books, demonstrates the way she trims the feet of her own Poodle named Gigi.

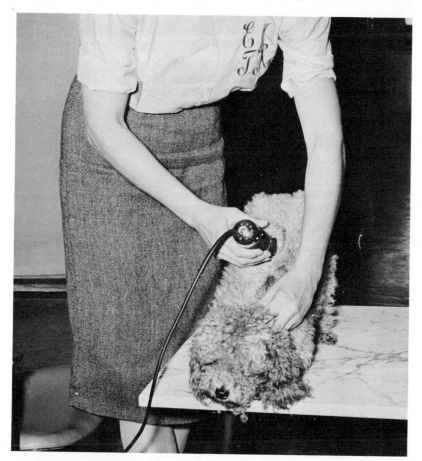

In executing a Dutch Clip, it is well to run the clipper blade the full length of the back from just behind the pompadour to part way up the tail.

Probably the most practical and least elaborate clip which you can dress your dog in is the Field or Kennel clip. With this style, the entire body, legs and neck are clipped at an even length, usually with the #5 or #10 Oster blade, or one of comparable size. As with all Poodle clips, there are many variations possible. For instance, with this style, you may have either full or tasseled ears. Also, the feet may be clipped very close, as with most Poodle clips, or the hair on them can be left at the same length as the rest of the body and simply rounded by a minimum of scissoring. The tail base, as usual, is clipped close and a moderately flat (about $2\frac{1}{2}$ inches deep) topknot is left which is blended gradually into the neck hair.

213

The tail should be clipped halfway down, as shown above. The illustrations show the best means of holding the tail when trimming top and bottom.

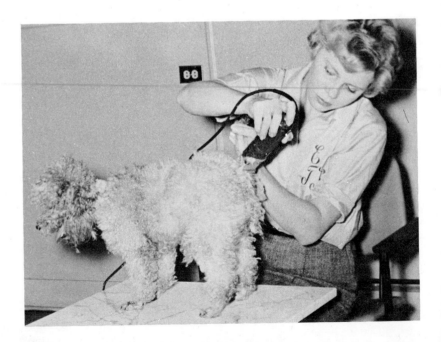

Above: By this time the puppy doesn't mind the grooming and may even enjoy it. Below: The tail tassel should be trimmed in the form of a ball.

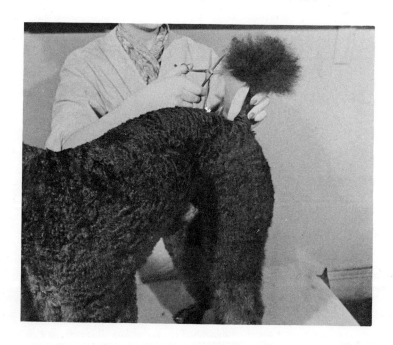

It takes a lot of patience to make a good tassel. Scraggly ends must be trimmed methodically.

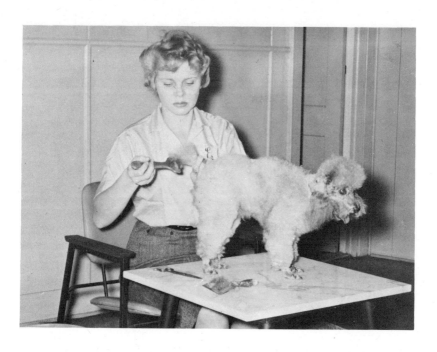

By combing and trimming alternately, the end result will be worth the trouble.

Above: This white puppy has learned to stand patiently and his grooming is almost over. The belly can be trimmed holding the pup in this fashion or it may be rolled over on its back.

The Dutch Clip. Courtesy of the Oster Co.

The Dutch clip. From the simplest clip we will progress to one of the more complex styles, namely the Royal Dutch Clip and its variations, the Dutch Clip. This clip, I might add, while it is not acceptable for show purposes, is without any question the most popular style today, and the one which most laymen think of when they consider the Poodle.

We will begin with the foot. A Poodle's foot should be completely and closely clipped. A #15 blade or comparable size should be used and the clipper should be directed *against* the grain—upward toward the body. All hair is removed in this manner, on and between the toes and pads. The feet should be clipped up to about a quarter of an inch above the dewclaw or

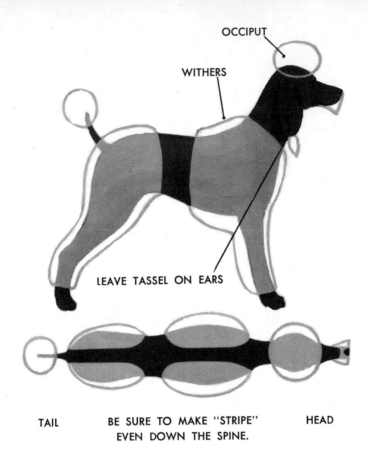

OCCIPUT

WITHERS

LEAVE TASSEL ON EARS

TAIL   BE SURE TO MAKE "STRIPE"   HEAD
              EVEN DOWN THE SPINE.

A schematic overview of the Dutch Clip. Courtesy of the Oster Co.

where the dewclaw was if it has been surgically removed. When you are finished clipping the feet, use a pair of scissors to trim around toes to remove any stray hairs you may have missed.

Next comes the face. Here you have the choice of clipping it clean or of leaving whiskers. If you decide to leave whiskers, you can make them as large or as small as you like. The usual manner of obtaining the shape is to lay the clipper flat on the top of the nose and run back from the nostrils to the eyes. The clipper is then placed on an angle and a line is established from the corner of the mouth to about a half inch behind the nostril. After this is done, the whiskers are brushed and shaped with scissors.

The ears may be finished in a variety of ways, but the most common way is to clip all hair off the inside and outside of the ears, with the exception of an inch or an inch and a half, which is brushed and shaped and forms the tassel.

When executing either the Dutch Clip or the Royal Dutch Clip, you may begin by running the clipper, with a #10 blade from the top of the neck, in a straight line, the width of the clipper blade, all the way to the base of the tail.

Next a strip must be clipped between the pantaloon on the front and rear legs. Usually on the Royal Dutch Clip this strip will only be about two inches, while on the regular Dutch the distance will be much greater depending on the size of the dog. This clipped area between the pantaloons goes all the way around the dog's mid-section and should extend slightly forward on the underside, toward the chest.

The upper parts of the pantaloons should be rounded so that a pleasant, well-proportioned pantaloon is achieved.

When you have completed the clipping and observe the dog from the front, the pantaloons should form a V shape with the lower part of the V being rounded and this should extend about one third of the distance from the Adam's apple to the dewclaws.

The pantaloons should next be brushed thoroughly with a wire brush and scissored. While scissoring, you will decide how full you wish the hair on the pantaloon to be. The length of this hair can be as short as one inch or as long as three or four. While deciding how long to leave this hair, it is well to consider the size of your dog and to try to clip in relation to this. Usually a small dog looks better proportioned if the unclipped areas are not left too full.

When clipping the face and ears to form the topknot a straight line from behind the eyes is drawn backward to a point where the ears are joined to the head and around the back of the base of the skull. The topknot is then brushed and combed and scissored to form a well rounded, moderately flat topknot. An inverted V is always clipped between the eyes and up the forehead about a half inch.

The Kerry Clip. The so-called Kerry Clip is done in very much the same manner as the Dutch Clip, except that the pantaloons are cut short above the elbow on the front leg and tapered down into the longer hair on the legs. The hair on the rear legs is tapered in the same manner as on the front legs and on a level with them.

There are many other clips and variations which you may want to try on your dog, and as you become more adept at handling your tools you will find this experimentation easier.

The English Saddle Clip. Courtesy of the Oster Co.

The English Saddle Clip. The feet are clipped closely about an inch or more up the ankle. At this point the bracelet on the front leg should begin and extend up the leg about two or three inches. The bracelet should be brushed well and scissored to roundness. The area above the bracelet is clipped to slightly below the elbow.

On the rear legs there will be two distinct bracelets. The first will run from where the feet have been clipped, about an inch or so up the ankle, to slightly above the hock joint. The second bracelet is started about an inch above the first one and extends up the leg to just a little below the knee joint. Above this second bracelet another band, about three quarters of an inch wide is clipped, all the way and parallel with the ground around the leg

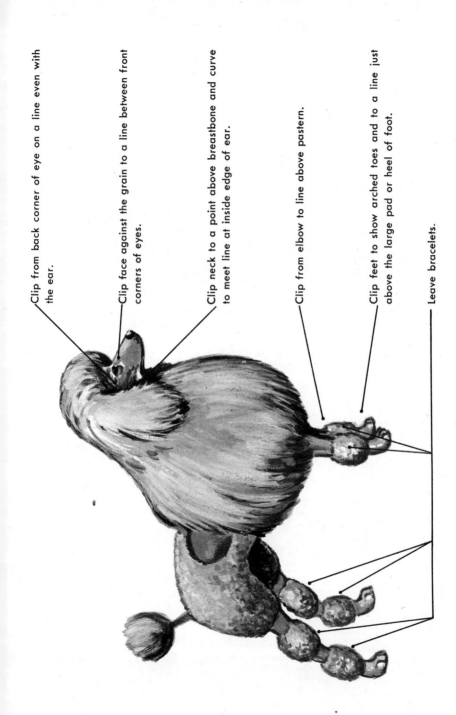

Clip from back corner of eye on a line even with the ear.

Clip face against the grain to a line between front corners of eyes.

Clip neck to a point above breastbone and curve to meet line at inside edge of ear.

Clip from elbow to line above pastern.

Clip feet to show arched toes and to a line just above the large pad or heel of foot.

Leave bracelets.

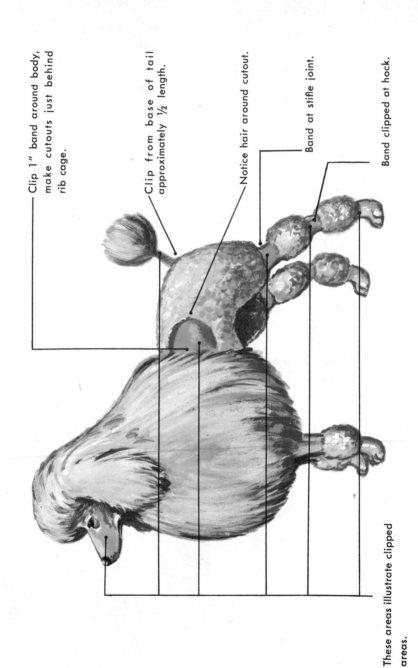

Clip 1" band around body, make cutouts just behind rib cage.

Clip from base of tail approximately ½ length.

Notice hair around cutout.

Band at stifle joint.

Band clipped at hock.

These areas illustrate clipped areas.

This little white rascal has been properly groomed at home and now he is being readied for the showroom and represents a vast amount of time and patience expended by his owner and handler.

to form the lower line of the "pack". The hair on the pack and rear bracelets is brushed and combed and scissored to about one inch long over-all.

The "pack" on the hind quarters is separated from the full hair on the front quarters by a one inch strip of clipped hair at about the last rib. This strip extends all the way around the dog and to the rear on each side, forming a crescent. The depth of this crescent will vary according to the size of the dog.

Aside from the clean-shaven face all of the rest of the head, ears and chest are left very full and only straggly hairs are removed. The tail, as usual, is brushed and scissored to a round ball.

The Continental Clip. Courtesy of the Oster Co.

The Continental Clip. The Continental Clip is identical to the English Saddle Clip from the last rib forward. The differences behind the last rib are as follows: The bracelet at the hock joint of the rear leg is about the same size and position as on the English Saddle Clip. The main differences between the two clips is that there is only one bracelet on each hind leg and there are two rosettes positioned slightly above and behind the kidney area. The rest of the hind quarters are clipped close. the rosettes are generally about two inches in diameter and circular.

The Puppy Clip. Courtesy of Oster Co.

The Puppy Clip. The Puppy Clip, which is acceptable in the show ring for puppies between six months and a year old, is accomplished by clipping the face, feet and base of tail in the manner previously described. The rest of the body and legs is merely scissored to an even, uniform length all over. The ears and topknot are left very full, only removing loose, straggly hairs with the scissors.

I hope that whether you perform your own grooming or have someone else do it for you, these pages will be of assistance to you in understanding the various styles and the means of achieving them.

Shedding

An outdoor dog who has no access to artificial light has a good shedding once a year, and that is all. A dog kept under artificial light part of every day may shed a little all the year round. Why?

Evidence points to the fact that the cycle produced by the changing length of the day is responsible for shedding. The coat comes out as soon as the days have lengthened materially, and is completed by August or earlier. The new coat grows, and by September has reached its prime, and is kept until next shedding season.

Remove this cycle's influence from the dog by turning on electric lights when the days are shorter, letting him stay in the home with you and go to sleep when you turn out the lights, and you have provided him with days of uniform length all the year through, except that some get light earlier in the morning and the dog awakens before you do. His shorter days are therefore of considerably longer duration than the outdoor dog's, and his long days are the same length. No wonder he sheds a little all the year round.

There is no other cure for this other than putting your pet in an unlighted room as soon as it is dark outside. Do that and the shedding will be only in early and midsummer. But you won't do that, nor would I, so just comb him frequently and he will not be a nuisance.

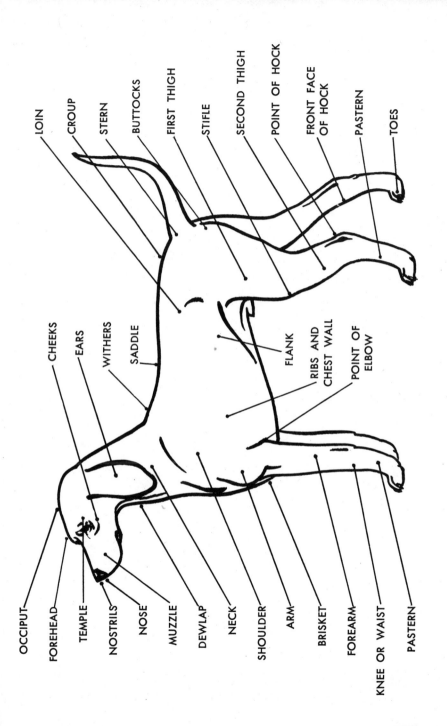

OCCIPUT

FOREHEAD

TEMPLE

NOSTRILS

NOSE

MUZZLE

DEWLAP

NECK

SHOULDER

ARM

BRISKET

FOREARM

KNEE OR WAIST

PASTERN

CHEEKS

EARS

WITHERS

SADDLE

FLANK

RIBS AND CHEST WALL

POINT OF ELBOW

LOIN

CROUP

STERN

BUTTOCKS

FIRST THIGH

STIFLE

SECOND THIGH

POINT OF HOCK

FRONT FACE OF HOCK

PASTERN

TOES

Index